CO-029

TROPICAL FISH

A COMPLETE INTRODUCTION

——Dr. Cliff W. Emmens——

TROPICAL FISH

A COMPLETE INTRODUCTION

Dr. Cliff W. Emmens

Front Endpapers: A school of *Cheirodon axelrodi,* the Cardinal Tetra.

The products illustrated in this book have been kindly supplied by the following manufacturers. Their appearance as illustrations does not indicate an endorsement, neither by the publisher nor the author. They have been chosen because they are internationally advertised and are available in the English-speaking countries of the world.

Aquarium Bologna (Mr. & Mrs. Pacagnella), Aquarium Pharmaceuticals, Aquarium Products, Diatom Filters (Vortex), Rolf Hagen Corp., Marine Enterprises, Marineland Aquarium Products, Penn-Plax Plastics, Inc., San Francisco Bay Brand, Inc., Second Nature (Willinger Bros.), Eugene G. Danner Mfg. Inc. and Wardley Fish Food Products.

The author wishes to thank the following for supplying excellent photographs to illustrate this book: Dr. H.R. Axelrod, Fred Eckler, Doug Faulkner, Michael Gilroy, Hilmar Hansen, Thomas Horeman, Burkhard Kahl, Dr. Karl Knaack, James Langhammer, C.O. Masters, Klaus Paysan, Hans Georg Petersmann, Helmut Pinter, Hans Joachim Richter, Col. J. Scheel, Gunter Schmida, Harald Schultz, W. Tomey, Gene Wolfsheimer and Ruda Zukal.

Distributed in the UNiTED STATES by T.F.H. Publications, Inc., 211 West Sylvania Avenue, Neptune City, NJ 07753; in CANADA to the Pet Trade by H & L Pet Supplies Inc., 27 Kingston Crescent, Kitchener, Ontario N2B 2T6; Rolf C. Hagen Ltd., 3225 Sartelon Street, Montreal 382 Quebec; in CANADA to the Book Trade by Macmillan of Canada (A Division of Canada Publishing Corporation), 164 Commander Boulevard, Agincourt, Ontario M1S 3C7; in ENGLAND by T.F.H. Publications Limited, 4 Kier Park, Ascot, Berkshire SL5 7DS; in AUSTRALIA AND THE SOUTH PACIFIC by T.F.H. (Australia) Pty. Ltd., Box 149, Brookvale 2100 N.S.W., Australia; in NEW ZEALAND by Ross Haines & Son, Ltd., 18 Monmouth Street, Grey Lynn, Auckland 2, New Zealand; in SINGAPORE AND MALAYSIA by MPH Distributors (S) Pte., Ltd., 601 Sims Drive, #03/07/21, Singapore 1438; in the PHILIPPINES by Bio-Research, 5 Lippay Street, San Lorenzo Village, Makati Rizal; in SOUTH AFRICA by Multipet Pty. Ltd., 30 Turners Avenue, Durban 4001. Published by T.F.H. Publications, Inc. Manufactured in the United States of America by T.F.H. Publications, Inc.

Contents

Choosing the right size, shape and location for your aquarium depends upon the room in which it is to be kept.

The Tank & Accessories

Choosing an Aquarium

The right sized aquarium for the beginner is clearly one that will enable him to keep a good assortment of plants and fishes without costing too much or giving unnecessary trouble. It mustn't be too big or it will be costly and difficult to service. It may even be too heavy for the floorboards. It mustn't be too small, or it will offer insufficient room for the inhabitants and will be subject to rapid cooling if not provided with a heater and thermostat, or if there is a breakdown of whatever heating arrangements it has.

All factors considered, an aquarium holding between 15 and 40 gallons is about right. A "high" tank is better looking than a double-cube arrangement, so that somewhere between 24″ × 15″ × 12″ and 36″ × 18″ × 15″ would fill the bill. The measurements given are length × height × width and the tanks quoted would hold 18 and 42 gallons respectively if filled entirely with water. A 24″ tank plus contents will weigh around 250 lbs and a 36″ one around 500 lbs, so they both need firm supports, but are not too heavy for a conventional sideboard or table if you decide to place them on the furniture. However, a special stand is often best.

We'll assume that you are going to purchase an aquarium and set it up with materials readily available at your local petshop and so shall not be talking about exotic designs— just a simple ordinary tank. The first thing to check is sound construction. Within the range specified, the glass should be ¼″ plate, with the bottom preferably of ⅜″ plate. Do not accept thinner glass in any tank

over 12″ deep, and do not accept scratched glass—both are faults that may lead to a burst tank. Older tanks were metal-framed and the glass was cemented in place with a special putty, but those offered for sale today are rarely so constructed. Any new aquarium will usually be of all-glass manufacture, but sometimes plastics may be used instead. The glass is held together with silicone rubber cement that forms a very strong but resilient bond and needs no supporting frame. Decorative strips may be added, but they are unnecessary. Make sure that the cement has been properly applied, with no bubbles or tunnels that may eventually cause a leak and that the tank is absolutely square—all angles must be 90° exactly.

Seventy-five years ago beautiful hand-made tanks and stands (usually one piece) were aerated with a hand pump and air storage reservoir.

All-glass tanks must be carefully supported, preferably on a flat even surface with ¼ to ½-inch of compressible material to ensure even support. This material must be waterproof, otherwise it will eventually become damp and troublesome. Styrofoam or other soft plastic foam is the best to use. Make sure also that the tank is completely horizontal, as any departure from this will show up when it is filled with water and annoy you for the rest of its existence in that position.

It is, of course, possible for aquaria to be of all kinds of shapes to fit special circumstances, or to provide unusual spectacles. There is a fad for very deep, column-like tanks with many-faceted sides that have necessarily to be made of thick glass. Should one attract you, remember that the water surface area is the most important factor in aerating the tank and that a deep tank can hold no more fishes than a shallow one of the same surface dimensions, even with aeration. Also, any tank deeper than the length of your reach can be a nuisance to service.

Covers & Hoods

Your aquarium will be fitted with cover glasses to protect the light, usually a fluorescent strip that will be placed over them, to stop fishes from jumping out, water from splashing and unwanted materials from dropping in. In any but the smallest tanks there will be a permanent strip of glass across the middle top to support the long sides. Strips below the edges of the tank will support the cover glasses. They are, therefore, countersunk a little. This arrangement stops water from running over the outside. The same objective can be achieved by plastic or stainless steel clips.

The cover glasses should have handles fixed to them for ease of handling, and allow for the insertion of heater leads and airlines at the back. A small segment in the front should

An ancient goldfish bowl made from hand-blown crystal with a rounded lip and a fashioned base. This type of goldfish bowl was the "rage" at the turn of the century.

allow for lifting off and feeding, but any well-made aquarium will have these things taken care of—just make sure they are! Cover glasses do not have to be as thick as the rest of the glass, but should not be unduly thin as they will no doubt be accidentally pressed upon or hit with something sooner or later.

It is a common design to have a hood covering the entire top of the tank, giving it a top-heavy look in my own opinion, and also needing an arrangement for getting at the cover glasses. My own preference is for reflectors covering only the light or lights and leaving the rest of the back and front accessible without the need for moving anything. Only very large freshwater aquaria need more than one top light and the size range recommended certainly doesn't, except for special purposes.

Lighting

Fluorescent lighting is now virtually standard for aquaria and has the great advantages of giving much less heat and more light per watt than incandescent lighting. It also offers a range of tubes that can provide types of illumination according to choice. Plants need the extreme ends of the spectrum for growth, especially the red, but it is not advisable to install special plant-growth promoting fluorescents as these are liable to give insufficient total light. Instead, warm white, daylight or "natural" tubes are best, or tubes that while giving adequate light also enhance the colors of the fishes. Take a good look around before you purchase and decide which suits your own particular taste. Your local petshop usually has special tubes made specifically for aquarium use.

Fluorescent tubes are usually rated at 10 watts per foot, so that a 2-ft tank with a single tube will receive 20 watts and a 3-ft tank, 30 watts. If on for about 12 hours per day, these amounts of illumination are just about right for the freshwater tank as long

Keep as far as possible to a lighting routine as the fishes become accustomed to this. A timer can be used, but avoid switching the light on in a dark room as it can lead to panic. Put the room lights on first and then the tank light at least a few minutes later. It is also best to reverse the procedure and not to plunge the fishes into sudden

Aquarium hoods hold the tubes/ bulbs that light the aquarium, and they also help to retard evaporation and keep dirt out of the tank. Photo courtesy of Rolf C. Hagen Corp.

This magnificent aquarium is used as a night-light. The lights are kept off all day and on all night.

as the tube runs the whole length of the aquarium. It is best placed more or less centrally, but for viewing the fishes you may choose to move it towards the front. If left there, it will encourage plants to tilt towards the front, so replace it in the standard position.

Breeding set-ups can be ordered through most petshops. The large tanks are used for spawning; the breeders are isolated in the smaller tanks on each side.

darkness as some species have night-time hiding places and should be allowed to settle down first.

Heating

No fish, whatever its natural temperature range, should be rapidly cooled or heated. An exception is that fishes that have been chilled do best if brought quickly to a normal temperature. Otherwise, a sudden downward change of more than 2°F and an upward one of more than 5°F within a short time must be avoided. At least a day should elapse during swings greater than these. These rules apply to coldwater fishes as much as to tropicals, for although many can live successfully over a wide range of temperatures, they cannot stand sudden changes.

Unless a tropical aquarium is in a constantly heated room, it must be provided with a thermostat and heater, usually combined in one instrument. This not only keeps the temperature high enough, but also prevents sudden drops when the outside air cools down. Even in the tropics such precautions are advisable, as a drop from 85°F to 80°F is just as dangerous as from 75°F to 70°F. For the same reason, a coldwater aquarium can with advantage have a thermostat and heater to prevent sudden drops in temperature.

Seasonal changes can be accommodated by varying the setting.

It is quite sufficient for the temperature to be controlled within 1.5°F and we don't want the thermostat to be clicking on and off too frequently and wear itself out.

Thermostatted heaters may be submersible, in which case they can be hidden behind rocks or plants but will have to be pulled up for any needed adjustments. The best have external controls

A 3-tiered aquarium stand.

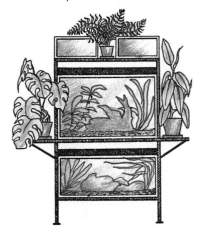

The heaters shown above and below range from 25 watts up through 300 watts and represent two different types of submersible heaters, adjustable (above) and pre-set. Photos courtesy of Rolf C. Hagen Corp.

so that it may not be too much of a chore. A pilot light is usually fitted to the thermostat so that you can tell if the heater is off or on—don't pull it out without turning the current off first even if it is off, as it may then switch on out of the water and cause trouble. The pilot light will also help diagnose heater failure. If the tank is falling in temperature when the light is on, the heater is not working and the equipment must be replaced.

There is not a wide choice of heater wattages. This means that instead of being able to choose one that nicely fits your tank's requirements, only something around the right wattage will be available. The right wattage is one that will just do the job, so that if by mischance the thermostat sticks in the "on" position, the heater will be incapable of cooking the fishes. Usually, a heater capable of raising the aquarium temperature 20°F above room temperature is ample, except in unheated rooms in winter in cold climates. Using this rule, a 24″ aquarium needs a 60-watt heater in theory, so a 75-watt heater will be the nearest available, or perhaps a 50-watt model if the room temperature can be relied upon not to drop severely. A 36″ aquarium in theory needs 124 watts—right in between the usually available 100 or 150 watts, so you can choose! Note that the larger the tank, the fewer watts needed per gallon, because the surface area where heat is lost is less per gallon in large tanks.

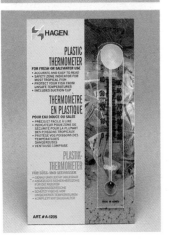

Naturally, you will need a thermometer. There are two types to be preferred—an internal floating or stick-on *alcohol* thermometer, not a mercury one in case of breakage and poisoning of the water, or an external stick-on liquid crystal type that indicates the approximate temperature of the water inside. It will normally read a bit low, perhaps by 2°F, but that can be borne in mind. A floating thermometer necessarily reads the temperature near the top of the water. Unless aeration is used, this may be a degree or two higher than lower down, as the warm current from the heater rises to the top. The others can be stuck inside or outside halfway down to give an average reading.

If possible, check your thermometer against a known accurate one, best done by sitting them side by side for an hour or so. Small errors of 1° or 2°F don't seriously matter and can be borne in mind, but any instrument worse than that (and some are) should be rejected. A tropical tank is best kept at 73°—77°F unless special fishes are present that do better at higher temperatures. Most species prefer the range cited to the higher temperatures at which they are often kept.

Three different types of aquarium thermometer: at top, a digitalized thermometer intended for attachment to the outside of the tank; center, a glass floating thermometer; bottom, a plastic thermometer equipped with suction cup for attachment inside the tank. Photos courtesy of Rolf C. Hagen Corp.

The Tank & Accessories

Aeration

Aeration allows the keeping of about twice the number of fishes that a given tank would otherwise safely hold, but this is not very often needed in tropical aquaria. Tropicals can be crowded if necessary—see your dealer's tanks—but few of us would want an aquarium to house such numbers. The fishes would not thrive eventually in crowded conditions. Aeration also mixes the water and prevents the "layering" effect described in the last section. What it does *not* do is to "force" oxygen into the water or do much to remove carbon dioxide. The water surface is the "window" of the aquarium and it is there that the most important gas exchange takes place. Aeration stirs the water and brings a constant stream up to the top where it flows across the tank and exchanges carbon dioxide for oxygen. Only uncomfortably brisk aeration adds much to this exchange by promoting gas exchange within the bubbles themselves.

Aeration is achieved with air releases at the bottom of the aquarium, supplied with air from a pump via plastic tubing. The usual device is an air-stone made of porous material, ceramic or other such

Beautifully molded plastic decorations such as this one serve as an aerator, an aquarium decoration and a wonderful place in which fishes can hide.

Aquarium decorations that depend on air from a pump for their operation must have the air channeled to them through airline tubing, such as the silicone-base Rolf C. Hagen Corp. tubing shown here.

substances, that releases fine bubbles. These should not be too fine, from $\frac{1}{30}''$ to $\frac{1}{50}''$ is best, or they do not move the water satisfactorily. Large bubbles just glug up to the surface and leave the water behind whereas very fine ones form a mist and are equally useless. Releases may be made of wood or even porous leather or other fabrics clipped into a holder, but these tend to give bubbles that are too fine and also tend to clog up easily. They are best avoided.

A pump is of course needed to provide the flow of air. One of the commonest complaints, even from neighbors, is about noise from an air pump. Quite powerful ones can now be obtained that are virtually silent, so be careful in choosing one. For a beginning

aquarist, a small diaphragm pump is the best and cheapest. Models are available that service up to a dozen or more tanks, but such a large pump will be unnecessary. Buy one that has a variable output. Purchase a non-return valve so that you can place the pump below the level of the aquarium if you wish, without risk of the water syphoning back if the pump fails or there is a power cut. Any noise that is still appreciable can be eliminated by placing the pump in a nearby cupboard. Individual flow into airlines leading to filters or other equipment, including other tanks, is controlled by gang-valves placed in the main air-line.

Vibrator air pumps are available in different sizes to suit varying demands for air output, but even the most powerful of vibrator air pumps don't draw much electric power. Photo courtesy of Rolf C. Hagen Corp.

Above: Battery-operated air pumps are very handy for providing air during transport, and they're excellent also as back-ups in the event of power failures. Photo courtesy of Rolf C. Hagen Corp. **Below:** Regardless of which type of air pump is used, vibrator or piston, valves that control the amount of air released to each air-operated device are needed. Inexpensive and reliable, air valves are easy to set up. Photo courtesy of Rolf C. Hagen Corp.

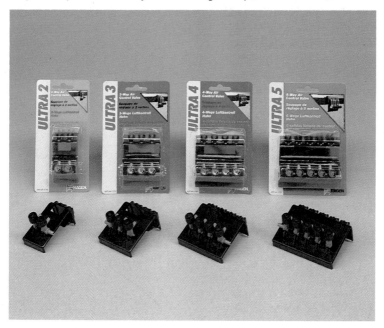

Filters

Filtration is by no means a necessity in a tropical freshwater aquarium, but it helps a lot if you are not able to service the tank as often as should be. It is almost a necessity if a goldfish tank is to be kept really clear, as they are very messy fish.

There are various kinds of filter mediums, from simple nylon threads or other plastic mats or staple, to activated carbon, resins or other materials designed to purify the water chemically as well as removing particulate matter. Old-fashioned glass wool is not used today as it splinters and may be a danger to both fishes and their owner. Plastic "wool" or filter pads only remove floating muck from the water, unless they are left in place for quite a long time, when they may develop some biological activity that we shall discuss later. Usually, the filter clogs up before this can happen and a clean replacement is necessary.

Activated carbon, or charcoal, is a popular material for removing more than just muck from the water. Do not accept shiny "coals" or any carbon that is not dull to look at and of pinhead size. This finely divided carbon has an enormous surface and can absorb up to half its own weight or even more of unwanted materials in solution. It should be sandwiched in between layers of plastic staple or mat, so that it is held in position and gross particles are filtered off before they get to it.

The carbon does several

Various forms of carbon are available at pet shops for use in some filters; the carbon filters impurities from the water. Photo courtesy of Rolf C. Hagen Corp.

This complete undergravel filtering system is magnificently illustrated in the photograph above. The adjustable air lift aerates the water as it pulls it from under the gravel. Special filter cartridges are available for attaching to the air stem.

things: it removes color from the water and keeps it crystal clear. It also removes some of the colorless toxic materials that otherwise accumulate and poison the water, including various chemicals that may have been added to cure or prevent diseases. If left long enough, it too will develop biological properties.

Sometimes a bacterial or algal bloom occurs in an aquarium that has been neglected or overfed, and this will not be easily dealt with even by carbon filtration. There are two main ways to deal with it in the absence of an undergravel filter, discussed later. Substances are available that cause the micro-organisms or other fine particles to clot together into masses large enough to be trapped in a simple filter, or a power filter may be used that forces the water through such a fine filter material that they are caught up by it. As such an expensive piece of equipment is unnecessary for the maintenance of an ordinary tank, the first method is to be preferred.

Left: Some filter media such as Biospheres by Rolf C. Hagen Corp. are used for both their mechanical and biological filtering properties.
Below: *Filter "wool" is relatively inexpensive and should be changed at regular intervals to maximize its efficiency. Photo courtesy of Rolf C. Hagen Corp.*

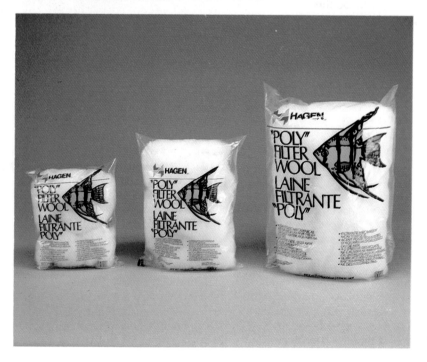

Other materials than activated carbon that may be placed in a filter include those intended to maintain a suitable pH (a measure of the acidity or alkalinity of the water) to absorb ammonia or other simple nitrogenous substances that may not be removed by carbon, or to soften the water. All have their uses in special circumstances but are not normally necessary.

The filter itself may be inside the tank or outside it. In both cases it is operated by means either of an airlift or a water pump. There are about as many designs as there are manufacturers, but for simplicity I shall describe three simple and perfectly adequate types of filter.

1. A plastic filter sits in a corner, hidden by decorations. It has a perforated lid through which the water flows down through the filter bed and through a perforated false bottom and then up through a central tube together with bubbles released by an airstone, or even just a jet of coarse bubbles. These form a lighter-than-water mixture and so the equipment works satisfactorily. Unsuitable for large tanks, it is quite good enough for smaller ones, up to about 20 gallons. It is an aerator as well as a filter.

2. Another type of inside filter hangs or is held by suckers at the top of the aquarium, projecting just above the water level. An airlift conveys water into the top of the filter box

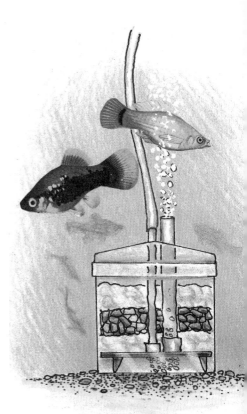

Above: A typical bottom filter. Water is sucked in through slits or holes in the top of the filter (not visible). Then water is drawn through various filter media such as glasswool, charcoal, etc., and then lifted from the bottom of the filter by air bubbles. Thus it aerates as it filters. Fishes like to play in the stream of bubbles.

Power filters that hang on the side of the tank, such as this power filter from Rolf C. Hagen Corp., provide a degree of aeration in addition to their filtering services, because when the water is reintroduced into the tank after having been filtered it creates beneficial water movement at its point of re-entry.

whence it flows down through the filter bed back into the tank via a perforated base. This airlift depends on the simple injection of bubbles into a plastic tube with a guard at the intake to prevent anything other than small particles from being sucked in. Such an airlift can turn over 25 gallons of water per hour, ample for most aquaria of the size range under discussion.

3. A very similar filter may be hung outside the aquarium, but in that case it must have a solid base and an arrangement for water intake and discharge. The intake is a simple inverted U-tube or tubes with a guard as before but no airlift. The discharge may be an airlift within the tank bringing water from the filter after it has passed through the filter bed, or a water pump,

usually called a power head, performing the same function. A power head, which may be submersible, can pump much more water than an airlift and is best in large aquaria or when rapid filtration is needed. All of the airlifts described, plus additional airstones within the tank, can be serviced by a small diaphragm vibrator pump.

Facing page, lower photo: Closeup of the airlift tube of an undergravel filter equipped with a carbon filter cartridge.

Cleaning of the aquarium gravel can be done a lot more easily through the use of one of the many siphoning tubes available for just that purpose. The large-diameter tube attached to a tube of smaller diameter allows the gravel to be lifted partially into the tube, where it is tumbled around and cleaned. After being cleaned, the gravel falls down the tube and back into the tank, but the unwanted debris, being much lighter in weight than the gravel, continues to rise through the smaller diameter tube and out of the tank. Photo courtesy of Rolf C. Hagen Corp.

Above: Power heads can be adapted for use as filters if provided with a retainer device to adapt the power head to straining out and holding particlute matter and a filtering medium (such as the Aqua Clear filter cartridge shown here). Photo courtesy of Rolf C.Hagen Corp. *Below:* Undergravel filters are available to fit all standard aquarium sizes. These Rolf C. Hagen Corp. undergravel filters are designed to fit 5½-gallon (left) and 10-gallon (tanks).

Undergravel Filters

Undergravel filters were first introduced for freshwater tanks, then taken up with great enthusiasm by marine aquarists because of their enormous capacity for purifying the water. Freshwater enthusiasts differ nowadays in their evaluation of such filters because some find that plants do not do as well in their presence. I shall present a method for using an undergravel filter that gets over this problem. It is possible in the freshwater aquarium because there is no need to cover the whole of the bottom of the tank as there is with marine aquaria.

The filter as now offered consists of a plastic plate with narrow slots and an airlift in one corner, held about ½" above the base of the tank by a series of supports. The gravel is placed over this plate to the usual depth of 2"–3". The airlift operates in

the usual manner to remove water from underneath the plate while replacement water flows down through the gravel, which acts as a filter bed. The slots in the plate should be $1/25''$ to $1/12''$ maximum in width, while the gravel, which must not pass through them, must be coarser. A mixture varying from about $1/10''$ to $1/5''$ or even larger in grain size is about right. As a precaution allowing the use of finer grains, I place a layer of plastic fly-screen over the plate before introducing the gravel.

When first introduced, the undergravel filter was triangular, with the airlift at a point of the triangle that was then placed at the center back with the triangle stretching to the center front. Such a useful design seems to have disappeared, but it can be substituted by placing the usual square or oblong plate available with the airlift at center back and the diamond formed by the plate extending to the front. Alternatively, you can cut a triangle from a large enough plate, but take care to tuck fly-

A cross-section of an aquarium shows the undergravel filter beneath the aquarium gravel. The terracing of the filter and its sloping from back to front can also be achieved by sloping the gravel.

screen over the raw edges so that gravel cannot get underneath. With these arrangements, the undergravel filter only operates where few if any plants need be rooted and so any disadvantage is avoided.

Both regular flow and reverse flow undergravel filters can benefit from the attachment of a power head. The Rolf C. Hagen Corp. power head shown here is for use with a regular (that is, the water flows down through the gravel bed) undergravel filter.

Densely planted aquaria offer an opportunity to conceal items of equipment such as airline tubing, filter stems, heaters, etc., that an individual aquarist might prefer not be visible.

To understand the workings of an undergravel filter we must enlarge a little on the meaning of biological filtration. In addition to acting as a mechanical filter, the undergravel filter houses a vast population of bacteria that consume some of the products of decay and metabolism in the tank. This population does not appear suddenly, taking characteristically about a month to develop fully, as the particular bacteria concerned are slow growing in comparison with others. The main eventual product of digestion and decay of organic substances in the aquarium is ammonia, which is toxic in fractions of a part per million (ppm). It is produced by the breakdown of feces, uneaten

Power heads are compact water-pumping devices; in addition to their filter-enhancing properties, they also provide very brisk water movement. Photo courtesy of Rolf C. Hagen Corp.

food, decaying plants and by the turn-over of bodily substances even in a starving fish. The more alkaline the water, the more poisonous is its ammonia content.

Ammonia is converted by bacteria of the genus *Nitrosomonas* to salts of nitrous acid—nitrites. Nitrites are also poisonous, although less so than ammonia, and are in turn converted by bacteria of the genus *Nitrobacter* to salts of nitric acid—nitrates. Nitrates are much less toxic than the foregoing and can be tolerated by fishes and other freshwater creatures in quite high concentrations up to 100 ppm or even more. However, regular water changes will stop the build-up of such amounts and a figure of 20 or 40 ppm is usually quoted as typical and safe. Plants also utilize nitrates and growing plants do a lot to keep the concentration down.

As other types of filter do not act biologically unless allowed to remain undisturbed for longer than is usual—because they clog up too quickly—the undergravel filter is a valuable addition to the tank. However, it doesn't do everything, in particular it doesn't remove pigments that gradually turn the water yellow. Unless considerable water changes are made, the yellowing of the water is best taken care of by a small activated carbon filter in addition to the biological filter. If medications are used, this filter is turned off temporarily and when in use again it will remove them from the water. An underwater corner filter is quite adequate for this purpose and so everything can be kept within the tank.

filters do an excellent job of cleaning the water, but they do not remove ammonia, nitrites nor nitrates. They are quite unnecessary with a single, small freshwater aquarium unless it is neglected or overcrowded, which should not happen.

You may even be offered a "minireef" type of aquarium, that consists of the main display tank plus a complex filter-aerator set-up in a cabinet below it, which ultra-purifies the water and gets rid even of nitrates. Whatever the virtues of such a system in the marine aquarium, it is again superfluous for freshwater tanks, and very costly. Try it if you have money to burn, otherwise forget it.

Although they're not filters, the various vacuuming and mulm-removing implements sold for use in aquariums—regardless of whether they're operated manually or by battery power or by an airstream—do a good job of removing sediment from both above and below the gravel, and their regular use helps to keep the tank clean. Photo courtesy of Rolf C. Hagen Corp.

Other Filters

You may be offered various expensive external filters, from hanging filters with various compartments, to power filters that sit beside or below the aquarium and pass the water through diatomaceous earth or capsules of various types. Power

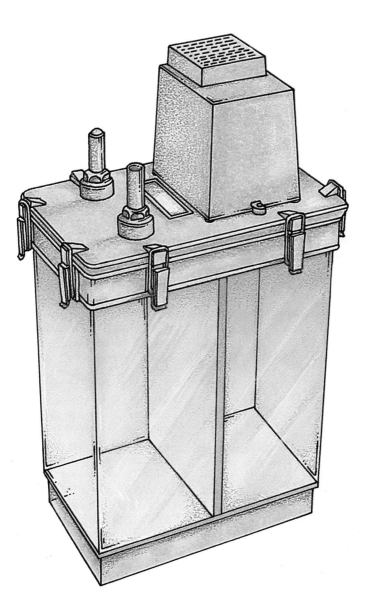

This canister-type outside power filter sucks water from the tank, forces it through a filtering medium in one chamber, then into a second chamber for further treatment or filtration and then back into the aquarium. They are only practical for larger aquariums of 20 gallons to as high as 500 gallons.

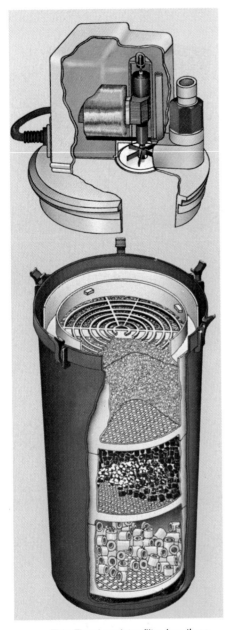

This Fluval canister filter has three chambers for mechanical, biological and chemical filtration.

Gravel

With an undergravel filter the grain size of gravel must be carefully chosen, as indicated above. Too fine or too coarse a gravel must be avoided with or without an undergravel filter. Very fine gravel, or sand, packs tightly and interferes with plant growth; too coarse a gravel allows food and debris to accumulate below the surface and cause trouble. However, a mixture of quite coarse gravel with some fine grains as well is acceptable, as the smaller grains pack the vacant spaces. With plants growing healthily, quite deep gravel rarely goes sour in the freshwater tank, even with no filter below it.

The nature of the gravel is very important. Unless you want a highly alkaline, hard water, as for some cichlids, lime-containing gravels must be avoided, so don't use shell-grit, coral sand or dolomite. Choose coarse river sand, silica sand or any neutral material, and see that it is very well washed before placing it in the aquarium. This may need many successive washings of ¼ bucket-full until no cloudy water runs off. Failure to do this invites trouble, as a gray cloudiness can result in the aquarium that is very hard to clear without a power filter.

Decorations

Some lime-free rockwork is often an attractive addition to the tank, so marble, shells or coral are out, as is any rock not guaranteed to be free of iron or other dangerous minerals. Driftwood or other well leached wood also offers decorative possibilities, particularly with fishes that come from areas where tree roots or dead branches are part of the natural scenery. It all depends on what you like; after all, an aquarium is there to please its owner; the fishes don't mind as long as it offers shelter and pleasant conditions.

Filter cartridges for the Fluval inside-the-tank canister filter can filter both particulate matter and liquefied wastes. Photo courtesy of Rolf C. Hagen Corp.

Plastic plants can be very natural-looking and certainly don't decay, but it must not be forgotten that they don't do anything except look nice. They don't mop up noxious materials or offer food for some of the fishes and they don't offer the pleasure of cultivating them and even selling superfluous stock. Growing plants that remain healthy are indicators of a healthy tank and help the aquarist to detect faults in

Canister filters that can be used inside the tank, such as the Fluval 2 model shown here, allow a number of different filtering media to be used for maximum efficiency. Photo courtesy of Rolf C. Hagen Corp.

33

Above: *Decorations intended for use in aquariums, such as these ceramic castles from Blue Ribbon, should be made of materials that can safely be used without harming the fish.* **Below:** *Plastic plants for use in aquariums come in many different sizes, forms and colors. Photo courtesy of Tetra/Second nature.*

management when they cease to flourish. There is such a beautiful range of aquarium plants available that it seems a great pity to be satisfied with living animals but not living plants.

Other plastic decorations offered are sea shells that open and shut as air bubbles into them, wrecked ships, divers, mermaids—there is an endless array. An aquarium is never exactly like a piece of natural waters transplanted to your living room, but there is no need to make it look highly unnatural—however, who am I to judge? If you really like such objects, put them in! I even recall a photograph of one pious lady's tank built like a chapel!

Nets are inexpensive but indispensable pieces of equipment for aquarists. Photo courtesy of Rolf C. Hagen Corp.

Auxiliary Equipment

Don't forget that you will need tubing, a syphon and a net, etc., as well as just the tank and its contents. Plastic air-lines should be soft and pliable so that you don't have a fight on your hands when putting them in position. Buy rather more than you seem to need as it is usual to find that something has been overlooked. Add a set of gang-valves so that the line from the air pump can lead off to the filter, air-stones, etc. and keep a spare air-stone with a generous length of tubing to aerate new water or newly purchased fishes.

As debris (mulm) accumulates, it will have to be syphoned off, normally at the time of a partial water change. Use a glass tube

Siphon starters allow siphoning action to be started without any need for mouth-to-siphon contact. Photo courtesy of Rolf C. Hagen Corp.

Pet shops sell aquarium gravel in many different colors in addition to natural-color gravel. Photo by Isabelle Francais.

A device for trimming and moving aquarium plants.

similar, perhaps slightly longer glass tube can also be used as a dip tube to suck up unwanted small objects or uneaten food. When you release the air, do so gently, or water will rush up the tube and splash over the top. Petshops offer many types of syphons, dip-tubes, etc.

The net or nets, it being much easier to catch out a fish using one in each hand, should be about half the aquarium width in size and made of soft synthetic material, dark green or brown in color. The larger the mesh size the easier to move it through the water.

Planting sticks, simple wooden or plastic sticks with a notch at the end, are very useful for replanting an established aquarium or replacing plants that

about ½″ in diameter and the same depth as the tank or a little longer, but not much. Connect it to a soft rubber tube several times as long and place a small length, about 2″ is enough, of the same rubber tubing over the business end to avoid chipping or breaking the tip. Plastic tubing is much harder to manage than soft rubber tubing when syphoning off the water. A

have floated up for some reason. A plastic, long-handled pair of pincers can be a great help when you don't want to plunge an arm into the tank. If you do plunge your arm in, be sure there is no soap or detergent on it!

Kits for testing water quality need only be confined to a pH test kit and perhaps a nitrite test kit, of use when first setting up a tank, but not really necessary. The pH kit should always be purchased and it pays to buy a good one. Avoid papers to dip into the water, they are often wrong; prefer a "comparator" type kit, with a sample of aquarium water compared with standard color tubes or glass slides, not colored paper. Discuss your water testing problem with your dealer.

Cleanup around the fish tank, whether the item being cleaned is the aquarium glass or any other part of the aquarium that might be subject to a buildup of mineral salts, demands the use of safe-for-fish cleansers like these from Python Products, Inc.

This syphon tube features a clear plastic or glass bell almost as deep as the tank, connected to a soft rubber tube. The syphon sucks old water and mulm out into a bucket (not shown). Petshops have wonderful syphon sets . . . or you can make your own.

Starting an Aquarium

You have bought everything you believe necessary to equip the aquarium, so how to go about setting it up? There are a number of logical steps that make the job easier.

1. Unless you are by nature artistic, make a diagram of how you propose to furnish the tank, as seen from front and top. Look over other furnished aquaria to see what effects can be produced and select one that pleases you as a guide, but don't copy it slavishly. Picture where everything, including the heater, air-stone and filter will go, see how they can best be made unobtrusive, and plan rock and plant placement. Select the rocks and plants after making these sketches, not before!

2. Wash everything thoroughly. The gravel and rocks, also the plants, can be disinfected with a solution of 3 ppm (⅕ grain per gallon) of potassium permanganate, leaving them for a day, or in a 7.5 ppm solution for 15 minutes, afterwards in fresh water. In an emergency, 15 seconds in sea water or 6 tablespoons of salt per gallon can be used. Wash out the aquarium with fresh tap water and clean all cover glasses and equipment similarly. Examine the tank very carefully so as to select the best front glass, free of significant scratches or other flaws. Sometimes the tank or its top are so constructed that there is no choice—so be extra careful before purchasing it in such a case.

Making a sketch before you start planting is advised. The two drawings shown above detail a top view and a front view.

Another type of aquarium layout. Stones and logs should be drawn to scale so you can truly appreciate the relative size in relation to the tank.

3. Make sure that the stand or whatever the tank is to sit upon is absolutely level, then place the styrofoam sheets or other suitable material in position and tape them firmly down or they may shift as you maneuver the aquarium into position. Two people should

4. (Optional, but strongly recommended.) Place the undergravel filter in position in the center of the tank, or somewhat to one side of center if you plan to have a large plant as a center-piece. If you have cut down a larger filter to suit requirements, remember to seal

Artificial plants have a number of advantages, but many hobbyists still prefer the real things for good looks and the over-all feeling of naturalness that they impart.

place the tank on its support, lifting it from below, not from the top or a supporting flange may crack. Check that it sits firmly in place and that you cannot even slip a knife blade under it anywhere. If you can, something is wrong, so start again. Did you make sure that the tank is square in the first place and that the stand is quite level and flat?

over any raw edges with the plastic flyscreen recommended as an extra precaution against gravel getting underneath. It is best if the front edge or corner of the filter is a little away from the front glass, so that it won't be visible later on.

5. Keeping it wet, place the gravel gently in position with a trowel or kitchen scoop, sloping

1

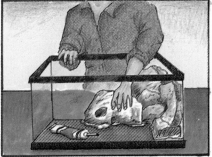

2

PREPARING A CICHLID AQUARIUM
Aquariums can be designed for many purposes. Cichlids, because of their habit of digging up the bottom, uprooting plants and undermining stone and logs, require a special aquarium. Once the aquarium is located and (1) the design has been decided upon, the raw materials (2) should be gathered. The stones, gravel, logs, and silicone aquarium cement. Heaters and filters come later.

The logs and stones should be glued in place (3) so they cannot be toppled and smash the glass as the cichlid digs underneath them. No further work can progress until the silicone aquarium cement dries and the stones and logs are firmly in place (4).

3

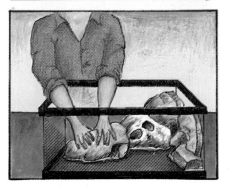

4

5

Once the aquarium cement has set, usually within 24 hours, work can continue. The gravel, after it has been thoroughly washed in hot and cool running water, can be poured into the aquarium (5) and shaped into roughly the terrain you have in mind. Usually the gravel slopes from the back to the front and from the sides to the middle. This will facilitate the accumulation of debris into a small area where it can easily be syphoned off. Then water is added (6) taking precautions not to allow the stream of water to destroy your sand sculpturing.

6

Once the water has aged for a few days and reached room temperature, you can add the living plants (plastic plants and ornaments don't have to wait for the water to age (7).

Then you can add the heater, lights, filters, hood, etc. (8). When the water is properly aged and reaches an acceptable temperature, fishes can be added.

7

8

it so that it forms a shallow basin with its lowest point at center front. It should be 3″–4″ deep at the back and at least 2″ deep in center front if an undergravel filter is used, otherwise it can be a little shallower, but not much. This arrangement assists the mulm to collect at the front for convenient removal and also looks nicer than a flat surface. If necessary, a few flat stones can be placed under the gravel at the

with a few stones to prevent them moving when the tank is filled. Do not allow the heater to touch the glass or to become covered by anything. It is a good idea to cradle it with a few small stones to achieve this end. Of course, if you use a model clipped onto the side of the tank this problem does not arise, but a bottom heater is best, less visible and more efficient, although more of a nuisance to get at if it needs attention.

Logs should be affixed to a firm slate base so they won't topple. A few holes in them provide hiding places for fishes.

back to conserve it, but leave enough depth for the plant roots, and don't use such a device with an undergravel filter. Terraced, sloping undergravel filters are great if you can find them.

6. Arrange all rocks and other decorations as desired, including the heater-thermostat, airstones plus airlines, and an inside bottom filter if used. Anchor all leads and airlines temporarily

7. Now is the time to fill the tank to the half-way mark. Run a hose into a small vessel placed inside the tank at center front, turn it on very gently and the water will spill over into the aquarium with minimal disturbance. It is best to run the hose briskly for a few minutes prior to this step, to clear away any stagnant and possibly contaminated water. If you

cannot use a hose, carry out the process with a watering can or tea pot instead.

8. Planting can now proceed. Trim the roots to 1″–2″ long since longer roots are very hard to deal with and will probably die anyway. If you are lucky enough to find them, only use potted plants which are already rooted. These are by far the best!

Tall plants naturally go to the back and sides, shorter ones in the middle and towards the front, unless you plan a center-piece that may be a tall plant, near mid-front. As a rough guide, a 40-gallon tank will need several dozen individual tall plants at the back and up to two dozen smaller plants, say five dozen in all for a nice planting. Use the

There is a special technique for planting. With a forefinger push the base of the plant into position from a site a few inches from the desired place and the roots will finish up under the gravel where you want them. Do not bury the crown of any plant such as an Amazon sword or it will rot. Pat the slightly disturbed gravel into place as a final step.

Like all living things, live plants need attention. The dead leaves should be removed and not be allowed to rot in the aquarium. As plants die, the fishes and snails usually start eating them, thus dying leaves are very evident.

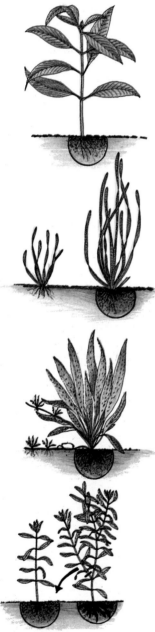

Try to get live plants with some gravel attached to their roots. This gravel will contain bacteria which is necessary for a successful aquarium.

planting sticks recommended for any accidents that happen after the initial stages.

9. At this juncture it is advisable to inoculate the aquarium with the bacteria that will be needed for the nitrogen cycle. They will always be present in small numbers, but to hurry things you can add a starter preparation available commercially, some gravel from an established *disease-free* tank, or even a few pinches of garden soil pushed down into the gravel. Although the toxicity of ammonia is much less at the typical pH— around neutral—of a community tank than at pH 8.0–8.3 of a marine tank, it is advisable to get the cycle going as rapidly as possible to avoid accumulation of the compound.

10. Now fill the tank to within about an inch of the top, or just under the supports for the cover glass, put the thermometer in place, cover glasses on and switch everything on. Leave it all going for several days, making any adjustments necessary, with the light on for about 12 hours per day—longer if you like. The thermometer with the heater operating should read around 75°F and not vary beyond 73° to 77°F. Any chlorine will have left the new water, but if your local supply includes chloramines (formed when ammonia is also added) treat it with a commercial neutralizer available from your petshop or add 1 grain per gallon of sodium thiosulphate.

Check the pH and if necessary adjust it to near pH

7.0 with a commercial kit or by adding small amounts of sodium bicarbonate to bring the pH up or small amounts of sodium acid phosphate to bring it down. What is a small amount? About one level teaspoon per 40 gallons, adding more if necessary until you get the pH right. A standard teaspoon holds 5 ml and it is best to use one of a set of calibrated cooking spoons that usually contains 1 dessertspoon (2 teaspoons), 1, $1/2$ and $1/4$ teaspoons, cheaply available in plastic. Ordinary teaspoons differ too much in size.

11. You can now start to add the fishes, but not all at once since the aquarium cannot take a full load safely at this stage. It will take several weeks for plants and an undergravel filter to operate properly. Start with some hardy species like the

Freshwater aquarium water conditioners such as A.C.T. by Mardel Laboratories can be used to reduce the buildup of organic pollutants in the aquarium.

Planter strips and pads are useful for anchoring rooted plants without adversely affecting root development; they also help to retain nutrients near the roots. Photo courtesy of Aquarium Pharmaceuticals, Inc.

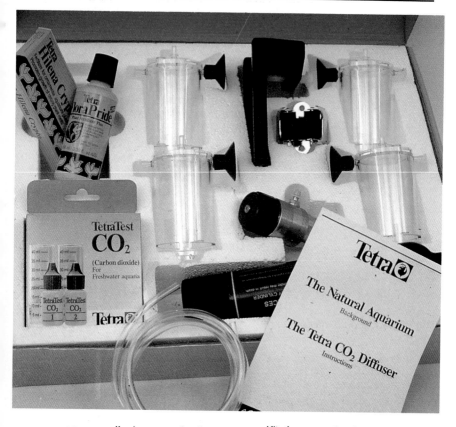

common livebearers, barbs, catfishes or loaches and add not more than a quarter of the calculated full load at first, with similar additions at weekly intervals. Leave the tenderest fishes and the most expensive ones (they often coincide) until last.

If you are in an out-of-the-way area and have to order your fishes by mail, or don't wish to pay frequent visits to a distant town, there is a way to overcome the difficulty. Instead of maturing the tank with live fishes, do it with a piece of rotting meat or fish and leave it for three to four weeks, measuring the nitrite

Kits for measuring the amount of carbon dioxide in the water and for supplying carbon dioxide to the water by means of a carbon dioxide diffuser can be helpful in maintaining maximum plant growth in the aquarium. Photo courtesy of Tetra/Second nature.

level every other day from day 10 until the peak has passed. The reading will rise from less than 0.25 ppm up to perhaps 10 ppm and then fall as the tank gets into its stride. Or you can use an ammonium salt. Ammonium chloride is best; add 2 ml per day of a 10% solution for every 25 gallons of water for the first 2 days, then 4 ml per day for the

Different fish can have different optimum pH ranges, so manufacturers have provided preparations that help to adjust pH factors automatically. Photo courtesy of Aquarium Pharmaceuticals, Inc.

next 2 days and so on until 10 ml per day is reached. Continue this until the nitrite peak has fallen to less than 0.5 ppm, stop medication and put the fishes in a day later. See the next paragraph for how many fishes the tank should hold.

12. Although aeration can about double the fish capacity of an aquarium, it is best to ignore it when calculating how many fishes to put in, or rather to regard it as a safety measure that allows for mistakes and growth. Don't be misled by your dealer's tanks; the fishes wouldn't do at all well if they spent an entire (but short) life in most of them. The window of the tank is its water surface and the fish capacity is calculated best from this. Here, then, are the surface areas needed by various sized fishes. They are naturally approximate, but will average out quite nicely in a community tank of mixed sizes and species.

Kits that permit aquarists to determine the amount of ammonia in their aquariums are widely available. Photo courtesy of Fritz Pet Products.

doubled for air-breathing fishes like gouramis and others possessed of a labyrinth (see below) and should be halved or even less for cold water fishes, especially fancy goldfish varieties. The fishes you buy will probably average around 2″ in length, so that a 24″ aquarium will hold about 24 fishes and a 36″ one about twice that number. Don't purchase fishes smaller than 1″ in length; most of them will be almost fry and need too much early care to flourish, plus lots of tiny live food.

Water conditioners designed to provide an increased protective coating to fish that have been subjected to stress as a result of handling or injury can be obtained at pet shops and tropical fish specialty stores. Photo courtesy of Mardel Laboratories.

Body length in inches (exclude tail)	No. of fishes per sq. ft. of water surface	Square inches needed per fish
1	55	2.6
1½	20	6.6
2	12	12.5
2½	7	20
3	5	30
4	2	65
5	1	120
6	1	180

Notice how rapidly the numbers per square foot fall as the fish size increases. This is because a 2″ fish has eight times the body weight of a similar 1″ fish, and so on, and is a reason why "inches per gallon" rules are less reliable and allow overcrowding of larger fishes.

There are two exceptions to these figures; they can be

13. Introducing new fishes to the aquarium is an art and must be aimed at minimizing any shock and stress, from changes in water quality such as hardness and pH to changes in temperature and aggression from other fishes. If properly packed and transported in an insulated container a new fish will arrive at a reasonable

temperature in a sealed plastic bag. Ask your dealer what the temperature and pH of his water is if purchasing locally and go elsewhere if he doesn't know. If the fish travels any distance, the pH and temperature will in all probability change. Measure them and take several hours over the next step if they differ very much from those of your aquarium   temperature by more than 3°F hotter or 5°F cooler, pH more than one unit. Otherwise take at least 1/2 hour.

Place each bag in the aquarium (I assume that you do not have quarantine facilities—if you have, use them), open it up and begin the water exchange. Using a baster or any large syringe, change about 1/3   of the water in the bag at intervals of not less than 10 minutes until it is mostly tank water—about 3 changes are minimal. With a large bag you can use a cup. If the temperature and pH differences are great, make the intervals longer. Watch how the other fishes behave towards the new ones and act accordingly— with any signs of aggression, be prepared to float the fish until the old inhabitants seem to lose interest, but don't forget that it needs water changes to survive, or an airstone.

Nets are relatively inexpensive but decidedly useful items for all tropical fish hobbyists. Photo courtesy of Rolf C. Hagen Corp.

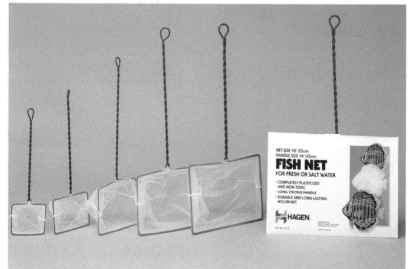

Water Checks

Hydrogen ion concentration (pH) is tested by a kit as mentioned on a scale of 0–14. Below pH 7 is acid, above it is alkaline and at pH 7 the water is neutral in reaction. Fishes live between pH 4.5–9.5, but nearly all are happy between pH 6–8. Those from waters like the Amazon prefer the lower part of the range and those from brackish or limey waters the upper part. In a mixed community of fishes, aim for pH 7, but don't worry about a gradual drift of half a unit. The usual pH indicator for freshwater is bromthymol blue, which is yellow at pH 6.0, green at pH 7.0 and blue at pH 7.6.

be maintained in the community tank. Soft water has a hardness below 100 ppm by definition, and hard water is above that figure. Up to 300 ppm is not uncommon in chalk or limestone areas. If your tap water is below 100 ppm, forget it. If it is much above that figure, soften the water or use an ion exchange resin—available at your petshop commercially in "pillows" to be placed in the filter.

Hardness kits can be purchased from your dealer, but he may have to get one in for you as many aquarists never worry about it.

Salinity is a measure of the salt, usually sodium chloride, content of the water. It really

Often a beginning tropical fish hobbyist can make a savings by buying a starter kit instead of individual items. Some kits contain the aquarium itself, whereas others contain only the equipment. Photo courtesy of Rolf C. Hagen Corp.

Hardness is a measure of the calcium plus magnesium content of the water, usually predominantly the former. Medium soft water is best for the general run of fishes and should

only matters if you are setting up a brackish water aquarium, as any water suitable for humans is O.K. in the aquarium except in very special circumstances.

To keep your aquarium looking fresh, clean, and attractive requires a rigid maintenance program. Daily, weekly, monthly, and quarterly routines are necessary.

A Safe Rule

Whenever you plan work on an aquarium remember the following: *It nearly always takes about twice as long to complete anything to do with a fish tank as you budget for it to take.* Something crops up—a pump seizes up, you discover that the filter is nearly clogged, the top covers need cleaning, when all that was planned was a 20% change of water!

Maintenance

Once an aquarium is a going concern it needs periodic maintenance. Just how much depends on how crowded it is and how liberally it is fed, but as a general guide the following checks and changes are desirable:

Daily Check the temperature and look at the fishes to see that all appear healthy. See that all equipment is working and that all covers are in place. Feed preferably lightly twice a day.

Weekly Make up for any evaporation, clean the glass and renew any box filter contents if necessary, usually only the top plastic mat will need attention.

Aquarium water changers allow water changes to be made without the need for the aquarist to siphon and add water manually. They are very useful devices where tap water is safe to add directly to the aquarium. Photo courtesy of Aquarium Products.

Use a water changer to change about 10% of the water over a period of an hour or two.

Monthly Syphon off about 20–25% of the water, taking the opportunity to suck up mulm. Disturb the surface gravel a bit to clean it. Replace with new, conditioned (previously stored) water at the right temperature. Cull any superfluous plant growth. After the aquarium has settled down, check the pH and correct it if necessary.

Quarterly Renew all carbon in the filter. Check all equipment rather carefully, replace clogged airstones and check all airline connections.

Never completely change the gravel, particularly over an undergravel filter. At most remove and wash one-third of it at a time.

Some Tankmates of Fishes

Some aquarists like to keep other forms of life than fishes in a community tank, although there are not very many choices in freshwater. Great caution must be exerted in doing so, as many insects and crustaceans will attack small fishes, carry disease, or be eaten by the fishes. The European great water beetle (*Hydrophilus piceus*) is an exception, large enough to escape predation and a vegetarian. Crayfish are safe with all but large and aggressive fishes. Vertebrates such as tropical newts and frogs *can* be kept with the fishes for a time, but don't live all their lives in the water. Turtles are OK with large fishes, but will eat small ones.

Snails may carry disease, but are safe if aquarium bred. Most feed on algae and detritus and leave healthy plants alone. Large snails such as the Japanese livebearer (*Viviparus malleatus*) may die and foul the tank and are best left out. Recommended species are:

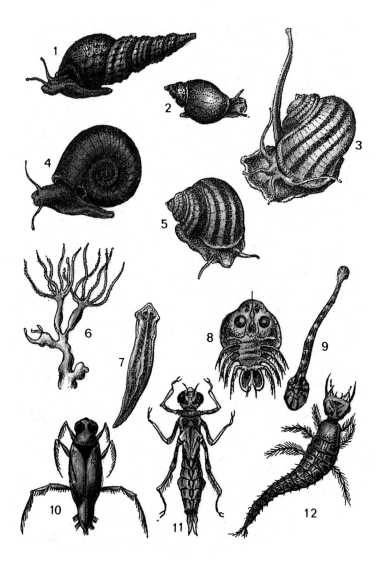

TANKMATES OF FISHES

As you add living plants or feed such live foods as Daphnia and other wild-caught feeds, you will probably introduce very small, inconspicuous things which grow into snails (1,2,3,4,5); Hydra which eat Daphnia and newborn fishes (6); planarian worms which may or may not bother your fishes (7); fish lice which attach to the outside of your fish (8) and can easily be removed from the fish with tweezers; leeches which attack both fishes and humans (9). These should be captured in a net and scalded before they are thrown into the toilet. Many aquatic insects such as diving beetles and dragonfly larvae (10,11,12) are dangerous and should be netted out.

Small freshwater crayfish are good scavengers but they also attack fishes.

The Malayan snail (*Melanoides tuberculata*), a small omnivorous snail that burrows in the gravel and keeps it clean. It is a prolific breeder and may be culled at night, when it emerges from the gravel.

The ramshorn snail (*Planorbis corneus*), growing as a flat coil up to an inch across, with an attractive red variety in a semi-transparent shell.

The Australian red snail (*Bulinus australianus*) is a small bright red whelk-like species.

Various *Limnaea* species, also whelk-like, some of which eat dead decaying flesh, but not living material.

Aquarium Plants

There is a tremendous selection available of aquarium plants, from algae to higher flowering plants. Some are still the original wild types, but many are domesticated or so-called horticultural varieties or hybrids. Some are even really land or bog plants that have been found to be suitable for aquarium use. As aquarium plants are rarely allowed to flower since to do this they most often shoot up out of the water, some have never been seen as flowers and their identity is uncertain. Very many plants cannot be assigned to a definite species unless the flower is available.

Plants help to keep the aquarium healthy because they use up waste products. For this reason it is rarely necessary to feed them; the fishes provide all that is needed. However, they only perform this function in adequate light and it is for the plants that there is a need for stronger light than the fishes require. Luckily different species have different requirements and some can get by with quite dull conditions compared with those needed by others, but the ones that tolerate dull lighting grow slowly and do not contribute much to the health of the tank.

What plants do *not* do is to contribute much overall to aeration, or rather oxygenation. In a good light they absorb carbon dioxide and give off oxygen that may be seen as tiny bubbles rising from the leaves in sunlight or very strong artificial

Your petshop will have magnificent aquarium furniture to show you. Not many stores stock luxury setups, but they can order them for you.

light. All very nice, but in poor light or darkness the reverse occurs, and they use up oxygen instead in ordinary respiration. So at night they compete with the fishes and are no help at all. All in all, it is best to ignore plants when thinking of aeration and to consider only the water surface, airstones and some types of filter.

Scientific Names

Like fishes, plants are classified into genera and species. A *genus* is a group of very closely allied plants and gives the *generic* name to each—e.g. *Sagittaria* or *Riccia*. A *species* defines each individual type of plant and the *specific* name follows the generic one—e.g. *Sagittaria subulata* and *Riccia fluitans*. Sometimes there are sub-species or varieties and a third name may be added to indicate this—e.g. *Sagittaria subulata* var. *gracillima*. After once mentioning the name of a plant, as long as there can be no confusion, it is usual to shorten it to *S. subulata* or *R. fluitans*. Above genera are families, orders and so on embracing wider and wider groups of plants until such large groups, called Divisions, as flowering plants, ferns and mosses, etc. are reached.

Unfortunately, there is a great deal of confusion about the names of plants offered in petshops, many being sold under the wrong name or as a species when really a hybrid. Perhaps it doesn't seriously matter except

Sagittaria subulata, forma gracillima.

Sagittaria subulata.

when an unsuitable species is offered under the name of a good one, but to the serious aquarist it can be a source of confusion and annoyance. Where possible, I shall indicate known sources of confusion. I should add that the source of most mix-ups is not your dealer, but his supplier or the botanists themselves.

Here, then, are some of the more popular aquarium plants that are readily available:

Strap-leaved Plants

Sagittaria subulata comes from the eastern U.S.A. and is a favorite background plant that comes in several varieties. *S. subulata* var. *gracillima* grows 1 to 3 feet in length and has long narrow strap-like bright green leaves at most ¼" wide. *S. subulata* var. *kurziana* (or *japonica*) is similar, but has wider leaves, up to ⅗" in width. *S. subulata* var. *subulata* is a much shorter plant, at most 4" long, and more suitable to the middle or sides of the aquarium.

S. graminea is another species offering several varieties, but they are less suitable for general use, not tolerating hard water and tending to break surface to form arrow-shaped leaves, from which the genus takes its name of arrowhead. All *Sagittaria* species propagate by runners that rapidly produce rows of new plants and all need good light to flourish.

Vallisneria species resemble

Sagittaria graminea *with flower.*

Sagittaria in size and shape and are equally valuable as background plants, needing similar conditions. Many of the plants now on offer are hybrids or of unknown origin so that it is difficult to give advice on purchases. Of known definite species, four are cultivated for aquarium use:

V. americana, from the southern U.S.A., has tightly coiled leaves about 1 ft in length and is commonly sold as *V. torta*. It does not tolerate hard water or cold water.

V. asiatica, from eastern Asia & Japan, also has coiled leaves, of a brighter green color. Unfortunately it is not always obtainable and is a slow grower in comparison with other *Vallisneria* species.

V. gigantea, from the Philippines and New Guinea, is as its name suggests, very large and suited only to big tanks. The leaves grow up to 6 ft in length and 1 ½" wide.

V. spiralis, a widely distributed plant, is not as spiral as the name suggests; the reference is to the flower stem and not the leaves. The leaves grow to 3 or 4 ft long and tend to clutter the top of the aquarium.

All *Vallisneria* species propagate as for *Sagittaria*.

Bunched Plants

Elodea nutalli, originally from North America, but now found in Europe, is a good aquarium species that is usually thrust into the gravel in bunches, where it develops roots and grows to

Left: Vallisneria spiralis, *so named for the spiral flower stem.* V. americana *on the right is truly spiraled.*

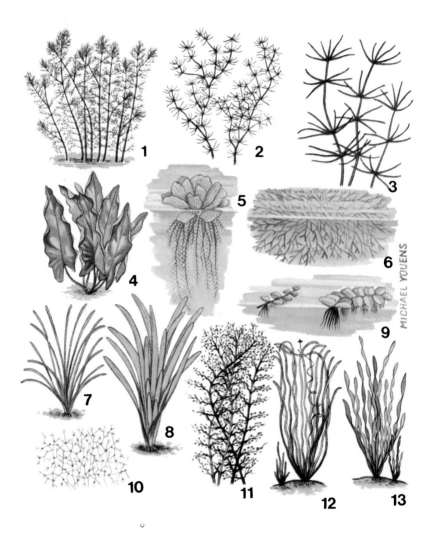

COMMON AQUARIUM PLANTS
1. Myriophyllum aquaticum 2. Nitella flexilis 3. Nitella megacarp 4. Nuphar sagittifolium, *the Cape Fear spatterdock* 5. Pistia stratiotes, *the water lettuce* 6. Riccia fluitans, *duckweed* 7. Sagittaria subulata 8. Sagittaria latifolia 9. Salvinia auriculata, *a floating plant* 10. Utricularia, bladderwort, *dangerous to fry* 11. Utricularia vulgaris, *another bladderwort* 12. Vallisneria spiralis 13. Vallisneria americana, *corkscrew val.*

about 5″ in height. It has whorls of ¼″ to ½″ leaves that curl over backwards and look very attractive. *E. canadensis*, with which *E. nutalli* is often confused, is not a good aquarium plant as it needs cool conditions and a lot of light.

Egeria densa, now found in many places but originally from South America, is a look-alike to *Elodea*, but has long stems up to 10 ft with whorls of bright green leaves. It can be kept under control by pinching off the tips frequently and replanting it in bunches.

Hygrophila polysperma, from India, is an old favorite with unbranched stems bearing light green leaves up to 2″ × ½″, in pairs. New leaves often have a reddish tinge. A rapid grower, it is usually pinched off as with *Elodea* and planted in groups.

H. corymbosa, from Malaysia, is a larger plant with leaves up to 5″ × 2″, otherwise similar to *H. polysperma*.

H. difformis, from eastern Asia, has finely divided leaves and is usually called "water wisteria." It is a very nice fern-like plant but does not do well in hard water or too bright a light.

There is quite a number of other *Hygrophilia* species suitable for aquaria, mostly of dubious identity so far.

Ludwigia species are placed in bunches in a rich substrate for best growth and appearance. Since the base of the stems deteriorates, pinch off the tops as growth proceeds and replant.

L. arcuata, from eastern

Egeria densa.

Hygrophila difformis, *water wisteria.*

Ludwigia palustris.

U.S.A., has reddish colored stems with emerald green leaves about 1″ × ⅕″, lance-shaped. It needs a good light and is then a fine aquarium plant.

L. repens has somewhat larger leaves than *L. arcuata*, comes from southern U.S.A. and has a horticultural variety "*L. mullertii*" that is redder and even larger.

L. palustris, the widely distributed species from all over the northern hemisphere, is similar to *L. arcuata*, but needs less light. All are good aquarium plants and hybrids between them make it difficult to know which you may be buying.

Myriophyllum is a genus with many species suitable for the aquarium, but does best in hard, alkaline water at about pH 8 and in good light. It is therefore less suited to the typical, soft and somewhat acid-to-neutral community tank. However, the plants are very attractive and worth a try.

M. aquaticum (Parrot's feather), from southern U.S.A., Central and South America originally, but now all over the place, is a favorite. The finely divided, light green whorls of leaves about 2″ long are on stems that grow up to 6 ft if allowed to do so.

M. mattogrossense is a similar but redder plant, from S. America.

M. spicatum is also very similar to *M. aquaticum*.

M. scabratum has thin green leaves and stems with lots of branches and is a popular species, found all over the northern hemisphere.

M. hippuroides and *M. ussuriense*, from the U.S.A. and eastern Asia respectively, have finely divided leaves and offer varieties from green to reddish-brown in color.

Limnophila is another attractive genus with finely-divided leaves in whorls on stems up to 3 ft long in the best-known species, but including other plants with undivided oval leaves. All do best in neutral to acid water.

L. aquatica from India and Sri Lanka likes a high temperature and is a very beautiful plant. It is commonly sold as *Ambulia*.

L. sessiliflora from all over tropical Asia is a more spidery plant that can stand lower temperatures and likes a dimmer light. It is the most commonly offered species and becomes light in color if exposed to too much light.

L. aromatica, also from tropical Asia, has undivided leaves and flourishes in a good light, but not direct sunlight, in which it yellows and ceases to grow well.

Cabomba is a genus of American plants that again have long stems, in this case usually branching and up to 10 ft in length. It has divided leaves in pairs along the stems, from which it gains the general name of fanwort.

Cabomba carolineana is a very variable and brittle plant, easily damaged, but attractive if grown under the right conditions. These are soft to medium hard water over 70°F. It may have tightly

Myriophyllum spicatum *with flower.*

spaced bright green leaves up to 3″ long, finely divided, or reddish leaves and stems, forming a very pretty plant. *C. carolineana* is often sold as *C. aquatica*, a similar plant that seems not to have been imported. *C. australis* is another very similar plant, but with smaller leaves about 2″ long.

Ceratophyllum demersum (hornwort) is found pretty well everywhere but is more a cold-water plant than suitable for tropical aquaria. It too has long branching stems and very brittle whorls of 2-pronged leaves. Attractive in the shop, but best left alone.

Left: Limnophila aquatica *with submerged and emersed leaves.* *Below:* Ceratophyllum demersum.

C. submersum differs from *C. demersum* in having 3-pronged leaves, but is equally unsuited to the tropical tank. There is a new, Cuban, unnamed species that has dense whorls and does well in warm water.

Individual Plants

The genus *Aponogeton*, from Africa, Asia and Australia, is represented by some 45 species and many hybrids. Commercially grown plants survive all the year round in the aquarium, although the genus is seasonal in the wild. Some species form rhizomes (thick, spreading root-like stems) from which new plants grow and can be separated.

A. crispus and its hybrids, often sold as *A. crispus*, have attractive, wavy-edged large leaves up to 1 ft long and 2″ wide. *A. crispus* itself has 1″ wide reddish leaves and the hybrids usually have green, wider leaves. The plants tolerate both soft and hard water, unlike a typical *Aponogeton*, and like bright light.

A. elongatus, from Australia, has less wavy leaves up to 15″ long on long petioles (stems). They are green to reddish in color. This plant is usually sold as a true species, but hybrids with *A. ulvaceus* are available. *A. elongatus* itself can stand cold water, but the hybrids cannot.

A. ulvaceus comes from Madagascar and is another quite large but very handsome plant. The long, curling light green leaves grow up to 20″ on 8″ to 12″ petioles, so need a large tank. Many so-called *A. ulvaceus* plants are dark-leaved, but are hybrids. This species and its hybrids have tuberous roots from which new plants develop.

A. undulatus, from Malaya, is also tuberous and has short-stemmed bright green crimped

Cabomba caroliniana.

Aponogeton ulvaceus.

leaves up to 15″ long in total, so not too large for a normal tank. Most plants offered are hybrids that look like the parent species but are better adapted to the aquarium.

A. madagascariensis, the Madagascar lace plant, is another large very showy plant, but hardly to be recommended as it is touchy, only lasts a season and needs frequent changes of soft, acid water. The blade of the leaf has holes between the veins and is about 8″ × 3″ in size, on an equally long petiole.

POPULAR AQUARIUM PLANTS
(1) Echinodorus parviflorus, *showing runners from a mother plant (2)* Echinodorus tenellus, *dwarf Amazon swordplant (3)* Echinodorus cordifolius *(4)* Eleocharis acicularis *(5)* Eleocharis vivipara *(6)* Elodea densa *(7)* Hygrophila polysperma *(8)* Lagarisiphon major *(9)* Lemna minor, *a floating duckweed (10)* Limnophila sessilflora *(11)* Ludwigia natans *(12)* Marsilea hirsuta, *the four-leaved clover.*

The genus *Echinodorus* belongs to the same family as *Sagittaria* and has many aquarium species, including the Amazon sword plants. It offers a range of attractive plants ranging in size from dwarf to very large, specimens of which are often used as center-pieces in large aquaria.

E. amazonicus is the small-leaved Amazon sword plant, from Brazil, with short-stemmed lance-shaped leaves up to about 6″ long. It does best in medium hard water and a high temperature, 77°–86°F, propagates by runners and rapidly populates the tank if allowed to do so. The young plants can be broken off readily. A nice plant for small tanks or as a carpet-former in large ones.

E. berteroi, from southern U.S.A. and Central America, is a very good aquarium plant with variable, bright green leaves that don't grow too large. They are ribbon-like at first, becoming oval and then heart-shaped as they grow. Its one drawback is a tendency to grow up out of the water if not stopped by nipping it.

E. parviflorus is a relative of *E. amazonicus* and resembles it, but is a lush plant with up to 50 leaves, lance-shaped with red-brown veins; a very attractive species.

E. maior, from Brazil, has light green leaves and looks like an *Aponogeton*, particularly if grown in rather poor light. It is a very handsome plant that grows happily in shade or brighter illumination and a temperature of 70°–77°F.

Echinodoras quadricostatus *variety* xinguensis, *a dwarf Amazon swordplant. This lovely mother plant is shown producing runners, each of which should be pressed onto the gravel so it can root and produce a new plant.*

E. quadricostatus var. *xinguensis* is the dwarf Amazon sword plant and has narrow green leaves up to 6″ long and ½″ wide. It reproduces rapidly from runners and will carpet an aquarium in no time. It is happy in any type of water and any temperature from 60°–85°F.

E. tenellus is really tiny, growing to less than 2″ high. Needing only a bright light and a

temperature of from 70°–85°F, it propagates rapidly by runners. It comes from the southern U.S.A. and Paraguay.

The genus *Cryptocoryne* provides a very large number of aquarium plants, many of which are hard to cultivate unless care is taken over water conditions. Typically, the water must be mildly acid, about pH 6.5, soft and clear. A sandy substrate with some peat or similar agent added and detritus left around the roots are also recommended. The lighting should be dull and the temperature steady between 70° and 85°F. Among the best for the beginner are:

C. affinis, from Malaysia, is a fast grower for a "crypt", with petioles and leaves each reaching 4″–6″ long. The leaves are emerald above, purplish below and spear-shaped. Reproduction is by runners, but the plant, quite unusually, often flowers below water with a lily-like blossom.

C. axelrodii, from Sri Lanka, is another vigorous plant and does well in medium hard water. The leaves and petioles are each about 4″ long, the former olive green above and reddish below. It may be sold as *C. willisii* or *C. undulata*, as the leaves are slightly crimped.

C. becketii, also from Sri Lanka, is a very popular plant, tough, resistant to adverse conditions and reproducing rapidly by rhizomes. The petioles are long and the leaf blades wide and short, up to 3″ only, olive brown above and pink or purple below. In strong light it becomes redder.

C. evae is of unknown origin. It is a very attractive large plant with leaves up to 8″ × 3″ on long petioles, dark green or brown on top and reddish to violet below. It can stand hard water.

C. nevillii, from Sri Lanka, comes as two cultivars (varieties), one with deep green oval leaves 3″ × 1″, the other with long strap-like leaves, green and about 4″ × ½″ or narrower. The petioles are short. Both are tough, rapid growers, tolerant of varied conditions.

C. parva is a dwarf species, probably from Sri Lanka, with narrow green blades about 1″ × ¼″ and short petioles of about the same length. It is easily grown from a stout rhizome.

C. tonkinensis from Vietnam is a large plant with reddish-brown leaves up to 16″ long and ¼″ to ½″ wide, with crimped edges. The petioles are short, making the species attractive as a background plant or a center-piece, as it is also reasonably tough.

C. walkeri, from Sri Lanka, is a medium-sized popular plant with green to brown leaves 4″ × 1 ½″ in size and petioles about 6″ long. Another tough plant, propagated by runners.

Ceratopteris thalicroides, water sprite, is a fern from various tropical areas, with deeply divided flat green leaves. It and the related but even more deeply incised and decorative *C. siliquosa* are poorly rooted but grow rapidly from nourishment in the water. Reproduction is

from offshoots that form rapidly in good light.

Floating Plants

Most of the plants that float on the surface of the water are fine for ponds, but more often than not are a nuisance in the aquarium. They block the light, stick up too much, and tend to grow very rapidly. Some, however, are useful at spawning time for those fishes that lay their eggs among the roots or stems, and for giving shelter to the young of live-bearing fishes.

Nitella flexilis, from all over the northern hemisphere, is a green alga. It reproduces vegetatively and forms dense mats floating in the water. It does best in hard, alkaline water and so is of limited use in most aquaria, but suits some of the livebearers. Other species of *Nitella* attach themselves to rocks or gravel and so do not float.

Riccia fluitans, or crystalwort, is a widely dispersed liverwort useful for spawning as it does well in soft, neutral-acid water. Thick masses of interlocked branching green spikes form under the surface of the water.

CRYPTOCORYNES
(1) and (2) Cryptocoryne nevillii *comes in two cultivars. One is a strap-like leaf as shown in fig. 1; the other is a deep green more oval leaf, shown in fig. 2* *(3)* Cryptocoryne beckettii *(4)* Cryptocoryne axelrodi, *green leaves with red backing (5)* Cryptocoryne cordata *(6)* Cryptocoryne haerteliana.

Top, left: Nitella. Bottom, left: Riccia fluitans. Above: Ceratopteris thalictroides.

72

The Fishes

There are many hundreds of species of freshwater tropical fishes that are easy or reasonably easy to keep and quite a number not so easy. Obviously the beginner should choose from the vast selection of easier ones, but we shall look at a few of the others as well, as some are among the most attractive available. As you are not going to indulge in too large an aquarium at first, it is also best to stock up with small species, so as to enjoy a good selection. It is a habit of aquarists to buy freshwater fishes in pairs, but not necessarily in sexed pairs. However, there is no need to do this unless you contemplate breeding them and the fewer of any one species you buy, the bigger the possible variety in the aquarium. Later on perhaps, you may wish to specialize and to keep small shoals (schools) so as to enjoy their habits or to select breeders. Beginning aquarists must depend on a knowledgeable dealer to help them select healthy, compatible fishes which they can afford.

Livebearers

Part of the family *Cyprinodontidae*, the livebearing fishes have arisen from the top minnows, that will be described later since they are not all easy to keep. In contrast, the livebearers are among the most favored and easy to keep-and-breed fishes. In many texts they are split off from the others

under the title of *Poeciliidae*. The young are born already well developed and able to swim to shelter. In a community tank few will survive, but it is easy to trap them and save some to grow up in another tank. Males are furnished with an organ called the gonopodium, with which they shoot packets of sperm into the females where internal fertilization takes place. The birth of young, up to around 200 in mature females of some species, occurs typically at about monthly intervals and several broods can follow a single fertilization.

A miniature aquarium containing a single, small goldfish and a few aquarium plants.

The guppy, *Poecilia reticulata*, from South America and Trinidad, is a domesticated fish today, having been bred and selected for decades, and very

The Fishes

few if any wild type fishes are imported, nor are they desired. All sorts of colors and finnage are available and although beautiful fishes can be purchased cheaply, show specimens can command high prices. It is a prime example, like the goldfish, of what can be done with inbreeding and intense selection for appearance and vigor.

Guppies may be the most well known of aquarium fishes. Wild guppies (above) show various patterns in the males, while the females are uniformly gray-green. Three of the photos at right show modern, cultivated females with more color than wild females: the photo second from top, right, and the four photos on the opposite page show males of various types.

The swordtail, *Xiphophorus helleri*, from Central America, is another old favorite, with a splendid sword in the wild-type male, and usually somewhat smaller swords in the many cultivated varieties of diverse colors and finnage. The female has no sword. The platy, *X. maculatus*, has no sword, but is otherwise a chunkier version of the swordtail, available in many varieties. Hybrids between the two species are common, so much so that few specimens of either can be guaranteed to be pure.

The mollies, originally called *Mollienesia*, hence the name, are now included in the genus *Poecilia*. The common molly, *P. sphenops*, is a short-finned fish of which the black variety is very popular. The sailfin molly, *P. latipinna*, is also available in black or in a variety of other colors, and has a large dorsal fin in the male, show specimens of which are magnificent. Both species, from south-eastern U.S.A. and Central America, require brackish, alkaline water to flourish and a vegetable diet, and so require somewhat different care from their relatives. However, both guppies and mollies can be adapted to sea water, although swordtails and platys cannot.

Barbs

Part of the family *Cyprinidae*, the barbs are old favorites, coming mostly from India and the Far East, as well as Europe and Africa. They were placed under

Xiphophorus helleri, *the red wagtail swordtail male.*

Xiphophorus helleri, *the red swordtail male.*

Xiphophorus helleri, *black swordtail female.*

Xiphophorus helleri, *black tuxedo highfin male.*

the genus *Barbus* originally, which has now been split up. They are easy to keep, colorful and usually peaceful fishes. Sex differences are frequent and so pairing is easy in most species. Like the rest of the fishes to be described, they are egg-layers but unlike some, take no care of eggs or young.

The genus *Puntius* contains the rosy barb, *P. conchonius,* available as short or long-finned fishes, the former being able to resist quite cold conditions

A pair of salt and pepper platies, still a popular livebearer.

whereas the mutant long-fins cannot. The black ruby barb, *P. nigrofasciatus,* is a beautiful fish, glowing with color, as is *P. sachsi,* a golden barb with red fins. The genus *Barbodes* offers the striped barbs *B. hexazona* and *B. pentazona,* the six- and five-banded barbs respectively, and the rather large *B. everetti,* the clown barb, as well as other attractive species. The genus

Above: Longfin black mollies. Right:
Puntius conchonius, the rosy barb.
Below: The black ruby barb, Puntius
nigrofasciatus.

Capoeta continues the striped varieties with C. partipentazona and C. tetrazona, the "banded" and tiger barbs, inclined to be fin nippers but handsome fishes, particularly the latter which is a very popular fish available in mutant forms such as albino and various body colors. Two other beautiful barbs are C. oligolepis, the checker barb and C. titteya, the cherry barb. The cherry barb is the only one I know that has produced young surviving by some miracle in a community tank!

77

The checker barb is popular but is becoming more rare as more colorful species and varieties of barbs become available. The checker barb, above, is known scientifically as Capoeta oligolepis.

To the right is the most common and popular of all barbs, the tiger barb, Capoeta tetrazona. The male is the lower of the two fish and has a redder nose, barely visible in this photograph.

This barb is the five-banded barb, *Barbodes pentazona*. There are barbs with 4, 5 and 6 stripes. They are all closely related though they are different species.

Danios and Rasboras

The danios, from India and the Far East, a small group of fishes, form another section of the *Cyprinidae*. All are worthwhile, active, slim-bodied fishes amongst which *Brachydanio rerio*, the zebra danio, is perhaps the best known, a small fish with horizontal black stripes or, in mutant form, rows of dots. A very easy fish to keep or breed. Its cousin, the pearl danio, *B. albolineatus,* is equally attractive and available in a golden variety.

The rasboras, genus *Rasbora*, mostly from the Far East, complete our mention of this family. They are more delicate fishes on the whole, but peaceful and often very attractive. *R. heteromorpha*, the harlequin fish or just "rasbora," is a very old favorite and lives well although small and unaggressive. *R. trilineata*, the scissortail, is not as colorful, it is active and easily bred. A favorite of mine is *R. einthoveni*, the brilliant rasbora, most attractive in schools, as are many of the genus.

Brachydanio rerio, *the zebra danio. The female is the upper fish. The male, the more slender of the pair, is shown below her.*

Rasbora heteromorpha, *one of the most beautiful and gentle of aquarium fishes.*

Rasbora trilineata, *the scissor tail rasbora, is the easiest of all the* Rasbora *species to induce to spawn because they have been bred in Florida for dozens of years.* Rasbora einthoveni, *shown below, is rarely spawned and is quite difficult to induce to breed.*

The Fishes

Neon tetras, Paracheirodon innesi.

Tetras

The tetras, a large group of fishes of the family *Characidae*, mostly from South America, were originally so-called because many of them were classified under *Tetragonopterus*, now abandoned. There are probably as many as 2,000 species, many of them good aquarium fishes, small and colorful. The easiest way to tell a tetra is the adipose fin, a small knob of fat rear of the dorsal fin. As many species are long-standing favorites, mutant forms are common. Under the

The head and tail light fish, Hemigrammus ocellifer.

The cardinal tetra, Cheirodon axelrodi.

modern trivial name of characins, these fishes offer a big selection of small, peaceful and hardy species, preferring soft, acid water, able to stand neutral conditions as in a community tank, but unsuited to harder or alkaline water.

The most famous of the tetras must be the neon tetra, *Paracheirodon innesi*, a beautiful little fish that defied attempts to breed it until it was realized that it requires very soft water. It has been eclipsed, but not replaced, by the even more brilliant cardinal tetra, *Cheirodon axelrodi*, a very similar fish. Other hardy and well-established

Leporinus fasciatus.

tetras are *Hemigrammus ocellifer*, the head and tail light fish; *H. rhodostomus*, the rummy-nosed tetra; *H. erythrozonus*, the glowlight tetra, another real beauty; *Aphyocharax anisitsi*, the bloodfin, does well in hard, even alkaline water and is an exception to the general rule for tetras. Finally, the famous piranhas, *Serrasalmus* species, belong to this family and most of them are quite dangerous to keep and are prohibited imports in many countries.

The bloodfin, Aphyocharax anisitsi.

Anostomus anostomus.

The family *Anostomidae* used to be classified with the *Characidae*. They comprise a few rather large fishes known as headstanders because of their typical head-down stance. The most handsome is *Anostomus anostomus*, the striped headstander, but it grows to 18″ and is not suited therefore to small aquaria. *Leporinus fasciatus*, the banded leporinus, swims in a normal way and does not grow quite so big, at any rate in captivity.

more colorful species such as *C. julii*, the leopard corydoras; *C. arcuatus*, the skunk corydoras; and *C. nattereri*, the blue corydoras. These are all 2″–3″ in size, but *C. hastatus*, the pygmy corydoras, is only half as big and swims up into the water off the bottom. Although these fishes are good scavengers and will root out tubificids from the

The bronze corydoras, Corydoras aeneus.

Catfishes

The catfishes belong to several families. The family *Callichthydae* of small stony-feeling armored catfishes is well known for the genus *Corydoras*, comprising very many often similar fishes. They come from South America and Trinidad and are peaceful, bottom-living fishes much in demand as scavengers. The bronze corydoras, *C. aeneus*, was the first to be widely kept, later displaced by some of the

gravel, they should be carefully fed and not left to exist on left-overs.

The upside-down catfishes, family *Mochokidae*, genus *Synodontis*, are a novelty, but in fact most other members of the genus are more attractive but swim normally most of the time. They are African fishes, of which *S. angelicus*, the polka-dot catfish, is a really attractive species, unfortunately rare and high priced, growing also to about 8″.

The polka-dot catfish,
Synodontis angelicus.

The family *Loricariidae* is South American, comprising a few rather large fishes in nature, but which can be kept smaller in the aquarium if bought young. They are mostly rather ugly but curiously attractive and useful as algae eaters. Well-known members are the sucker catfishes that cling to plants or the glass of the aquarium, such as *Otocinclus arnoldi*, Arnold's sucker catfish, that grows only to about 2"; *Hypostomus plecostomus*, the sucker catfish, that grows to 2 feet; and *Loricaria parva*, the whiptail catfish, a rather colorless but nicely ugly fish growing only to about 4". Other species grow, in general, far too big for smaller tanks.

Loaches and Botias
Those members of the family *Cobitidae* suitable for aquaria mostly come from the Far East and are typically bottom-living fishes that act as scavengers, but should be catered for as well when feeding. The best known are the coolie loaches, lumped together because they are often confused. *Acanthophthalmus kuhli*, the true coolie loach, has full vertical dark bands along the body; *A. semicinctus*, the half-banded loach, has bands on the top half only; *A. myersi*, the slimey Myersi, has very broad dark bands; while *A. shelfordi* has broken bands. In very densely planted aquaria, these fishes occasionally produce unexpected young.

Otocinclus arnoldi, *the sucker catfish.*

aggressive. We come now to families containing many members that fail in one respect or another to fulfill these criteria, although other members are perfectly acceptable.

Hypostomus plecostomus, *the sucker catfish.*

(Facing page) Top: Botia macracantha, *the clown loach. Center:* Botia modesta.

Botia sidthimunki.

Acanthophthalmus kuhli.

Acanthophthalmus semicinctus.

The botias offer some very attractive fishes. The most spectacular is the clown loach, *Botia macracantha*, that like many of its kind does best in small swarms. *B. hymenophysa*, the banded loach, *B. modesta*, the orange-finned loach, and *B. sidthimunki* ("Why call a loach 'Sid the monkey,' daddy?") are all worth having, although the first-named, like the clown loach, can grow large, up to around a foot in nature.

Most of the fishes so far discussed are inexpensive, easy to keep and neither too large nor

Top Minnows

Part of the family
Cyprinodontidae, so-called
because of their habit of keeping
to the top of the water among
plants, the top minnows, most in
the genus *Aphyosemion*, are
beautiful and sometimes touchy
fishes. They lay adhesive eggs
that may take many weeks to
hatch and can be dried without
being killed. They have been
hybridized extensively but rarely
to advantage and it is best to
seek true species. *A. ahli*, Ahl's
lyretail, is one of the most

Above: Aphyosemion ahli. *Left:* Aphyosemion bivittatum. *Below:* Epiplatys dageti monroviae.

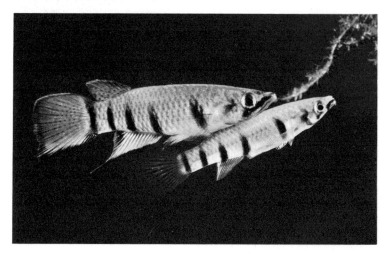

Cynolebias bellotti

beautiful and comes in various color strains; *A. australe*, the lyretail panchax, and *A. bivittatum*, the two-striped aphyosemion run it close, the latter best kept on its own. *A. australe*, however, has quite drab females but splendid males. The list could be continued with another twenty or more species, many best kept on their own and not for a beginner's mixed tankful. Similar comments apply to *Aplocheilichthys* species, but *Aplocheilus lineatus*, the striped panchax, is a hardy and pretty fish.

Another group of African top minnows is the genus *Epiplatys*, with some pretty and hardy members. *E. dageti*, the red-chinned panchax, formerly *E. chaperi* and often sold as such, is an old favorite, while there are other equally nice species, but beware of keeping them with any fish they can swallow. Over to South America, and we encounter the annual fishes, mentioned only for curiosity. These fishes of the genus

Cynolebias, of which *C. bellotti*, the Argentine pearl fish, is best-known, are short-lived little fishes that lay eggs in water holes that dry out seasonally. For some parts of the year no fishes exist, only eggs, which hatch out with the next rains.

Cichlids

The family *Cichlidae* has some of the fiercest yet popular species, many of which grow large and are not for the community tank. Others are quite small and peaceful while some, although peaceful, are large and for the specialist. There has recently been an influx of dozens of new cichlids from African lakes, previously unexplored commercially, and some are spectacular, but for the specialist again. The cichlids are distinguished for caring for the young, not that some other fishes do not do so, but the whole family goes through a similar routine of looking after eggs and young very meticulously.

One of the longest kept species is the angel-fish, *Pterophyllum scalare*, from South America. It is a domesticated fish, in the sense that it has been tank bred for many years and is available in many mutant forms, black, golden, lace, long-finned, veiltail and others. Angels should be maintained in neutral to slightly acid, clear water.

Discus fishes, genus *Symphysodon*, also from South America, have been kept for fifty years, but until recently were expensive. Now they can be purchased young quite reasonably priced, although prize specimens still command very high prices. They are for the specialist and are mentioned mainly because of their habit of feeding the young by secretions of the skin—a fact that hindered breeding in captivity for a long time until it

Long-finned angelfish, Pterophyllum *species.*

Hybrid blue discus with fry, Symphysodon discus.

was discovered that eggs and young must remain with the parents.

Cichlids that may be kept in a community tank with little or no trouble are the dwarf species, mostly of the genera *Apistogramma* and *Nannacara*. They are nearly all peaceful and grow only to about 2 ½″. The butterfly or ram cichlid, *A. ramirezi*, is a beautiful multicolored fish, actually timid rather than aggressive, doing best in slightly acid, soft water, with plenty of live food. *A. agassizi*, Agassiz's dwarf cichlid, has similar requirements. *A. reitzigi* is an attractive, real dwarf, rarely attaining 2″ in length. There are about a dozen other species, some of which are best kept on their own. Among

An Apistogramma ramirezi *golden female laying eggs.*

the *Nannacaras, N. anomala*, the golden dwarf cichlid, is an attractive, peaceful species.

Pelvichachromis pulcher, the kribensis (originally *Pelmatochromis kribensis*), is not classed as a dwarf, but it grows little bigger and makes a fine aquarium fish, absolutely beautiful, peaceful and inexpensive. The striped kribensis, *P. taeniatus*, is equally desirable, both doing well in typical community conditions. These are African fishes, in contrast to the dwarfs that come from South America.

Relatively peaceful "normal" cichlids include *Cichlasoma meeki*, the firemouth, a

Apistogramma reitzigi *(left).*

Apistogramma agassizi *male.*

spectacular fish growing only to about 4″ and *C. festivum*, the flag cichlid, that grows a little larger. Most other *Cichlasoma* species are pugnacious and large. *Aequidens pulcher*, the blue acara and *Hemichromis bimaculatus*, the jewel cichlid, may attract attention because of their spectacular colors, but be warned, they are rogues. The

Above: A drawing showing two male firemouth cichlids, Cichlasoma meeki, *with their gill covers extended, preparing to battle. (Facing page) Top:* Pelvicachromis pulcher, *female. Center: A pair of* Nannacara anomala *spawning. Bottom:* Pelvicachromis taeniatus *with their spawn. The male is the uppermost fish.*

The Fishes

The flag cichlid, Cichlasoma festivum.

orange chromide, *Etroplus maculatus*, from India and Sri Lanka, stays small and attractive and is usually peaceful enough to be a community fish, but its relative *E. suratensis*, the banded chromide, must be avoided. It is aggressive and can grow to 16″. Both require a little salt in the water, 1 or 2 teaspoons per gallon, which does no harm to other fishes but can be hard on plants.

Aequidens pulcher *preparing to spawn.*

Etroplus maculatus.

Hemichrom is bimaculatus.

its own kind, is the famous Siamese fighting fish, *Betta splendens*. Long-finned and gorgeously colored males may be kept singly with other fishes, as may several females, but two males will go at it hammer and tongs and completely rip each other to bits. The females are short-finned but may be of almost any color, as may the males, but are never so intensely colored as the males.

Anabantids

The anabantid fishes possess an organ called the labyrinth in the gill region, in which air gulped at the surface can be stored and utilized by a plexus of blood vessels. This enables them to inhabit foul water, for which purpose they also build nests of bubbles at the water surface, usually guarded by the male.

One of the first exotic fishes kept in temperate areas was an anabantid, the paradise fish, *Macropodus opercularis*, that can stand cold water, coming from China and Taiwan. It is a quarrelsome but handsome fish, quite unsuited to mixed tanks. Another fighter, but only towards

The paradise fish, Macropodus opercularis.

The Siamese fighting fish, Betta splendens, *male.*

The gouramis are peaceful and beautiful fishes from the Far East. The three-spot gourami, *Trichogaster trichopterus* comes in a blue variety (var. *sumatranus*) that outshines the wild type and is a beauty, but it gets rather large, up to 6″. There is also a smaller, golden variety that is much prized. The pearl gourami, *T. leeri*, is equally beautiful in a subdued manner—

The pearl gourami, Trichogaster leeri.

just silver, violet and black in a lacy pattern. The kissing gouramis, *Helostoma temminki,* a pinkish-colored fish, and *H. rudolfi,* grow large, but are kept for their interesting habit of kissing each other, purpose unknown. Alright for a year or two, but they do grow quickly. A real gem is the dwarf gourami, *Colisa lalia,* growing only to about 2". The male has blue and red vertical markings that have an enameled look.

Kissing gouramis kissing, Helostoma temmincki.

The blue or three-spot gourami, Trichogaster trichopterus.

The dwarf gourami, Colisa lalia.

Oddities

There are some fishes, quite suited to the community tank, that you will see on sale from time to time, that are worth keeping for reasons of beauty, curiosity or weirdness of one kind or another. They crop up in different families and so will be mentioned in alphabetical order.

Badis badis badis, the dwarf chameleon fish from India, is a bit shy, but a pretty little fish with iridescent colors. It grows to about 3″ but is usually offered much smaller. Not really much of an oddity, but rarely seen.

Badis badis, *the dwarf chameleon fish.*

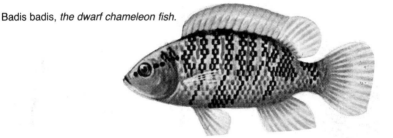

Butis butis, the crazy fish from the Far East, is a goby with a big mouth that doesn't seem dangerous to smaller fishes however. It spends its time cleaning rocks and plants and swimming upside down. Its maximum size is about 6″.

The crazy fish, Butis butis.

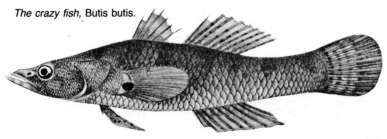

Gasteropelecus sternicla, *the silver hatchetfish.*

Carnegiella marthae or *C. strigata*, the hatchetfishes, have deep compressed bodies and wing-like pectoral fins. They must be kept in well-covered tanks or may jump from the water. *C. marthae* grows only to 1 1/2", *C. strigata* to 3". Both come from South America and should be given mosquito larvae and weaned in part onto floating dry foods.

Chanda baculis, the smallest of the glassfishes, from India and Burma, is practically transparent, growing only to 2". It is the best of the genus for a mixed tank, and it does well in soft water.

Epalzeorhynchus kalopterus, the flying fox from Sumatra and Borneo, is a pretty fish that eats algae, but is also omnivorous—a useful combination. It may grow to 4", but is usually smaller.

Garra taeniata, the Siamese stone-lapping fish, is an inhabitant of fast-flowing streams that does well in the aquarium and eats algae. As it is an attractive fish, it is well worth picking up if available.

Gasteropelecus maculatus, the spotted hatchetfish and *C. sternicla*, the silver hatchetfish, are further freshwater "flying fishes" similar to the *Carnegiella* species and suited to the

The marble hatchetfish, Carnegiella strigata.

Chanda baculis, *the smallest of the glass fishes.*

Epalzeorhynchus kalopterus, *the flying fox.*

Garra taeniata, *the Siamese stone-lapper.*

The glass catfish, Kryptopterus bicirrhis.

community tank. Like the others, they are South American fishes growing to 2"–2 1/2". *G. maculatus*, however, is a difficult fish to feed, demanding live food at the surface of the water.

Kryptopterus bicirrhis, the glass catfish, does best in small groups, but has been kept singly quite successfully. It is another transparent fish, peaceful and best given plenty of live foods. A close relative, *K. macrocephalus*, is less transparent. Both are from the Far East.

The red-tailed black shark, Labeo bicolor.

Labeo bicolor, the red-tailed shark from Thailand, is a beauty—black with a red tail. *L. erythrurus*, the rainbow shark, from the same locality, has reddish fins as well. Both are liable to fight among themselves, but not with other fishes. They can grow to 5″, but are usually available much smaller, and prefer slightly alkaline water, rather hard, although I have kept *L. bicolor* in a soft water tank quite successfully.

Lepidarchus adonis, the adonis from Ghana, is a fish that would be transparent but for deep black markings, quite an oddity, growing only to about 1 ½″, and liking soft, acid water. Feed it on live foods at first.

Melanotaenia maccullochi, the dwarf Australian rainbow fish, is attractively colored and grows to about 2 ½″ maximum. It is a hardy, interesting and lively fish, well worth having. Other *Melanotaenia* species from Australia and New Guinea are larger, but some are very colorful and most are easy to keep and breed.

The adonis from Ghana, Lepidarchus adonis.

Melanotaenia maccullochi, *the dwarf Australian rainbow fish.*

Labeo erythrurus, *the rainbow shark.*

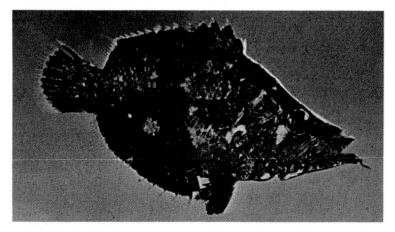

Monocirrhus polyacanthus, the leaf fish, from South America, is a real oddball. Drifting in slow streams, it looks just like a dead leaf, even to a mid-vein and stalky looking lower lip. It will swallow small fishes, so can hardly be recommended for a community tank unless your fishes are all reasonably large. It usually only eats live foods.

Nannostomus marginatus, the dwarf pencil fish from South America, is the most popular of its genus, but others are fine too, and not much bigger in most cases. *N. marginatus* gets to only about 1 1/4".

Monocirrhus polyacanthus, *the leaf fish.*

Notropis hypselopterus, the sailfin-shiner, is a native of the U.S.A. and a beautiful fish with, however, rather dull females. Coming from the south, it can stand a tropical aquarium, although it is said that a cooler period each year is an advantage. It grows to 3".

Pantodon buchholzi, the butterfly fish, is an insect-eater from West Africa, but can be trained to take other foods. It is so unusual in appearance as to be worth trying, but should be kept with fishes that are unlikely to nip its filamentous pelvic fins. It grows to about 4".

Pyrrhulina vittata, the banded pyrrhulina, is from the Amazon and tributaries and makes an attractive addition to a community tank. *P. spilota* and *P. brevis* are also worth having if you ever happen to see them for sale. All grow to about 2 1/2".

Nannostomus marginatus, *the dwarf pencilfish.*

A top view of the butterflyfish from Africa, Pantodon buchholzi.

The sail-fin shiner, Notropis hypselopterus.

Pyrrhulina spilota.

Scatophagus argus.

Rhadinocentrus ornatus.

Rhadinocentrus ornatus, the southern soft-spined rainbow fish from Australia, is an active, pretty fish not growing too large, up to 3″. A little salt in the water helps to keep it happiest.

Scatophagus argus var. *rubifrons*, the red spotted scat or tiger scat from coastal Indo-Pacific waters, is a beauty and lives well in slightly salted water since the juveniles, the desirable stage at 1″–1½ ″, come from estuaries that are almost fresh. It stays small for a long time if not overfed, but be prepared to pass it on since it can grow to 2 feet

or so eventually. Mentioned because of its real attractiveness, whereas the usual spotted scat is colorless in comparison. In contrast to some other authors, I have not found it to be a plant eater.

Selenotoca multifasciata, the silver scat, has similar requirements and does not grow big—up to around 4″ only. It comes from the same waters.

Tanichthys albonubes, the white cloud mountain fish from China, comes long and short-finned, growing to about 1 ½″. It comes from a restricted area around Canton and at one stage, when it appeared to be fished out in its native streams, they were restocked from aquarium bred specimens.

Selenotoca multifasciata.

Telmatherina ladigesi.

Telmatherina ladigesi, the Celebes rainbow fish, is a real beauty, requiring a little salt in the water—about 1 teaspoon per gallon. It looks best when mature, at about 3″, and when given live foods.

The white cloud mountain minnow, Tanichthys albonubes.

Foods and Feeding

Fishes are very good at assimilating food, much better than we are, so that an adequate amount of food to keep them healthy and not growing too fast may seem very little to the beginner. However, they require a diet rich in protein and low in saturated fats, which they poorly digest. A dry food should contain at least 45% protein if intended for tropicals and at least 30% for cold water fishes in a cold climate. Live foods or frozen foods contain a lot of water and so are naturally lower on a percentage basis, but the equivalent dried content is what matters. A good diet also contains some vitamins, particularly of the B group and

Commercially prepared fish foods come in many different forms; flakes, pellets, granules and pastes are just a few of those forms. Shown are pellets. Photo by Isabelle Francais.

vitamin C, as like ourselves, some fishes cannot manufacture their own. Special foods for species that need plant material will fall short of the stated requirements, but that is an exception and they will usually eat some of the other foods as well.

Flakes
Flakes have a special place in today's menu for fishes and there must be more of them fed than anything else. A good flake can supply a pretty adequate diet for the average fish, but should never be the sole item. Supplement them with frozen or live foods at least occasionally. Sometimes the color of the flake indicates its contents, but usually it does not and is there to attract the customer and not the fish. A flake should be reasonably thick, not wafer thin and crumbly, should float on the water at first and then gradually sink and not cloud the water.

Granules and pellets
These foods can contain ingredients like pieces of insects, plants or other materials not incorporated into flakes, and be suitable for some of the larger and more voracious species. They are made suitable for carnivores, vegetarians or omnivores. As with flakes, a list of ingredients is usually given, but there is rarely an indication of how much of each is present, so depend more on the protein content than anything else—and hope that it is at least predominantly first class protein.

Freeze-dried Foods

These are good, because you know what is in them and if they have been properly prepared they can offer the best value for money. Freeze-dried krill, for instance, can contain up to 65% protein and is an excellent food—not as a staple, but for frequent feeding. Other good varieties are brine shrimp, bloodworms, tubifex and various "planktons," some of which are suitable for very small fishes. All should be varied with other diets—never stick to a single type of food since we just don't know enough to be sure that any one food is fully adequate on its own.

Frozen or Canned Foods

Most materials available as dry foods can also be purchased frozen or canned, predominantly the former. Those sterilized by irradiation are safest, unless you stick to items like brine shrimp or other shrimps that come from salt water. You can in fact make up your own diet from canned foods intended for human use, avoiding anything fatty or oily. A mix of canned crab or lobster, vegetables such as spinach, shrimps, fish, oysters, or the same in deep frozen form, chopped to suitable sizes is excellent. Wash it free of unwanted sludge and juices and freeze in ice cube trays. It is much easier, however, to use commercially prepared, nationally advertised fish foods.

Above: Freeze-dried blackworms above, freeze-dried krill below. Photo by Isabelle Francais.

Right: Flake foods are available in many different sizes; the canisters shown represent only two of the sizes in which Nutra Fin Staple Food flakes are available. Photo courtesy of Rolf C. Hagen Corp.

Foods and Feeding

Other "Kitchen" Foods

European aquarists are fond of feeding their fishes on chopped ham, beef heart or other meats and report excellent results, despite their content of saturated fats. Many fishes certainly like these items, but it would seem unwise to give much of them, even of fish itself. Heart contains a toxin, meats cause digestive troubles and raw fish destroys some of the vitamins in other foods. As a change, feed some of the above by all means, but not too often.

Some fishes like bread, and an occasional feed of crumbs of wholemeal bread, or of small chunks to larger fishes, is appreciated, supplying roughage, minerals and vitamins.

Live Foods

Now that satisfactory prepared foods are available it is not necessary to feed live foods except in certain circumstances,

Live tubifex worms.

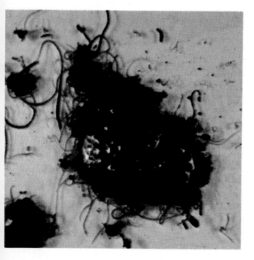

such as for breeding some species or raising the young. However, live foods are much appreciated and help to maintain good health. Young fishes need them to grow and thrive and as many shops sell quite juvenile stock it always pays to supply live foods to them. These are available at your aquarium shop. Live adult brine shrimps, *Daphnia, Tubificid* worms, white worms or mikro worms being commonly stocked. Some, such as white worms, mikro worms and brine shrimp are easily cultured at home.

White Worms

The white worm is *Enchytraeus albidus*, a small round worm about 1″ long found in damp, dark places where some form of food is available, such as under garbage bins or flower pots. Clean soil in plastic boxes, enriched by adding milk and any baby food or porridge in small pockets can be used for cultivation. Cover this with a glass sheet and then an opaque top cover and store in a cool place. On removing the latter, you can see the worms around the food and they usually stick to the glass in sufficient quantities. Add new food every few days. Cultures are available at specialist aquarium shops.

Grindal Worms

A smaller species of worm was first cultivated by Mrs. Morten Grindal. It is about ½″ long and likes a higher temperature than the white worm, around 70°– 75°F, and may be cultivated by

Live white worms, magnified.

the same method using peat for preference instead of soil.

Mikro Worms
These are very much smaller worms and are probably *Anguillula silusiae*, found in soil and growing only to about 1/10". They bear tiny living young that are a useful first food for fish fry. Feed the worms only to small fishes, even the adults, as larger ones ignore them. Cultivation is in shallow plastic boxes with about 1/5" of any cooked

Earthworm.

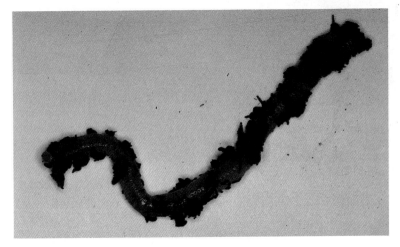

BRINE SHRIMP

(1) Eggs, hatchlings (nauplii) and adults (2) To hatch them successfully, you need a gallon jug, an air pump, an air stone, sea salt, and, of course, the brine shrimp eggs (3) More than one jug can be set up. Just add some eggs. Follow the directions since many eggs have different origins and different hatching methods (4) Temperature plays an important part in hatching. The eggs must be constantly aerated in the most violent aeration possible (5) Turn off the air, allow everything to settle, and use a flashlight or other light source to attract the nauplii. Then net them out. Wash off the salt (6) before you feed them to freshwater fishes (7) Use the net to release them into the tank. The fishes will love them (8) If you want to grow them to size, use a large, aerated tank which gets direct sunlight. Add some brewer's or baker's yeast.

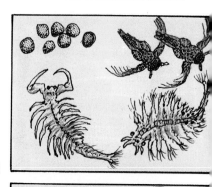

1

2

Harvesting live brine shrimp from California brine ponds. Photo by Hans J. Mayland.

3

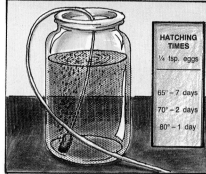

HATCHING TIMES
¼ tsp. eggs
65° – 7 days
70° – 2 days
80° – 1 day

4

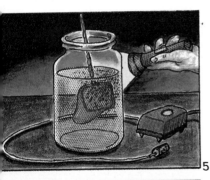

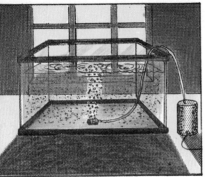

breakfast cereal, without salt but with milk. When cool, add a little baker's yeast and of course, some worms. Then stack small sticks of water-logged wood in criss-cross tiers that sit up out of the food for two or three layers and cover and keep dark at up to 80°F, the warmer the better. The worms collect on the sticks and on the sides of the container. Set up a series of cultures as it is not profitable to keep any one going for very long.

Brine Shrimp

Eggs of the brine shrimp, *Artemia salina*, can be stored dry for years and still hatch out in salt water. They may be purchased either in their natural state or shelled, the latter costing much more. A small vial can contain millions of eggs. These hatch out in sea water very conveniently, or in a 3.5% solution of common salt in water (about 4 oz per gallon, or 7 heaped tablespoons). Use butcher's salt or the pure chemical, not table salt. Kits may be purchased for hatching and collecting newly hatched shrimps, or you can use one of the two following methods for eggs in the shell:

Method 1: If a small quantity, say up to a mere 100,000 of eggs is to be used, take a shallow pan holding ½–1 gallon of salt water and carefully float up to ½ teaspoon of eggs per gallon on the surface. Cover and keep at not less than 70°F; 75°F is better, and leave for about 2 days, when the young will hatch out into the water, leaving the egg shells on top. Dip a flexible syphon into the water and run off through a very fine cloth to collect the *nauplii*, the larval shrimps. With care, no egg shells will be collected. Wash the shrimps with fresh water and feed to any but large fishes. The salt water can be used several times.

Method 2: If you want more *nauplii*, use gallon glass containers and fill ¾ full. Put in an airstone and use up to one teaspoon of eggs per gallon. Aerate very briskly and after 2 days at 70°F or over, turn off the air and wait for ½ hour. Some shells will float, others will sink, but the *nauplii* will swim free in the water and can be syphoned off as before.

Shell-less eggs, that come suspended in a preservative liquid, can be hatched by either method, but sit on the bottom if method 1 is used. After hatching the water can be poured through a cloth to harvest the *nauplii*. Details of how many eggs are to be found per drop or per ml of suspension are given on the container or leaflet that goes with it—usually about 2,000 per drop; 40,000 per ml; or 1 million per oz.

Raising Brine Shrimp

The *nauplii* will survive for several days after hatching, but must be fed and transferred to a stronger brine if they are to grow. For San Francisco brine shrimp, a brine consisting of 10 oz of common salt, 2 oz of Epsom salts and 1 oz of baking soda (sodium bicarbonate) per gallon of water is appropriate. This is alkaline and about twice

the strength of sea water. Put only about 500 *nauplii* per gallon into the brine if you intend to raise them all, more if to use them part-grown, and aerate briskly. Feed on baker's yeast, just a few pinches well stirred in at first, to be renewed as the water clears. Cover to prevent evaporation. At over 70°F, the adult stage is reached in 6–8 weeks and the culture will then be self-sustaining. However, it will only stand moderate culling, and new cultures should be started at intervals if a good supply of adults or semi-adults is needed.

Foods from the Wild

There are many foods you can collect for yourself, although some are also available in petshops. Many insect larvae are excellent foods, but those that are predators must be avoided, such as dragon fly or water beetle larvae. These are usually at the bottom of ponds or streams and can be left there. There is also some danger in introducing wild materials into the freshwater tank, so all catches should be washed in tap water before use.

Mosquito Larvae

Various mosquito species lay egg-rafts on the surface of the water, looking like floating granules of soot. Each hatches into tiny "wrigglers," air-breathers that grow to about ⅓" over the course of the next 8 or 9 days, turn into comma-shaped pupae, the equivalent of a butterfly chrysalis, and then hatch into mosquitos—a stage to

Live adult brine shrimp, Artemia salina. *Photo courtesy of San Francisco Bay Brand.*

Foods and Feeding

be avoided. Up to then, they are fine fish foods that do not use up oxygen in the water and so can be fed in excess. Collect them with a fine net, sort for sizes with sieves if you wish, and store in screw-topped jars in the refrigerator.

Chironomus
This is the "blood worm," the larva of a gnat, red in color and quite large at up to 1″ long, food for the bigger fishes. They live deeper in the water than mosquito larvae, so be careful of predators when collecting them. *Chaoborus*, the "glass worm," is a colorless edition of the blood worm, found in colder waters.

Daphnia
The water flea, *Daphnia pulex*, is the commonest available crustacean used for food and found in fresh water. It swarms in reddish to greenish masses in warm, but not hot weather, the color depending on its food and the particular strain of fleas. Store them as for mosquito larvae. They can be fed on liver powder, dried blood or other protein-rich foods, but are difficult to culture unless in large vessels—50 gallons or more, and kept cool, as they tend to die off above 70°F.

Other Crustaceans
Moina, Diaptomus and some other small crustaceans may be collected as is *Daphnia* and can also be bred. Some fishes will not eat them, but most will. Avoid *Cyclops*, with her one eye and two egg sacs, as most fishes

don't like them and they can be a pest in the aquarium. Larger crustaceans such as *Asellus, Gammarus* and *Hyallela* may be collected from ponds or streams and are much appreciated by the bigger fishes. They can be bred, the first two in cold water, *Hyallela* in warm water as well, treated as for *Daphnia*.

Tubificid Worms
These worms, sold under the name of *Tubifex*, are of various species that live in foul conditions. They are seen as red to brown waving masses at the bottom of sluggish, polluted streams, where they feed on filth and wave their tails to collect oxygen. Individual worms are 1″ to 6″ long. It is easier to buy them than to collect them, but if you do collect them they must be thoroughly cleaned. Even bought ones should be cleaned as a precaution. Place them in a vessel under a dripping tap and break up the masses into which they will gather. Do this periodically for a day or so until there is no visible muck or dead worms. They can then be stored in the refrigerator (spouse permitting!) and washed again before use. It is not feasible to culture them. Fishes are very fond of these worms and they are sometimes the only food that a new fish will eat at first. It is not good to feed them too frequently or freely as they are very fatty and can also establish themselves in the aquarium.

Earthworms

Earthworms are good fish food, whole to big fishes and chopped up for smaller ones. They can be stored in damp leaf mould and even bred in it, but it is easier to collect a few or to buy them if large quantities are needed. They may be brought up from a lawn by pouring a solution of 1 grain per gallon of potassium permanganate over it.

Feeding

The appetite of a fish depends primarily on temperature, so in the tropical tank it remains steady and good. It will fall with very high temperatures or lack of oxygen, that tend to go together. Small fishes cannot eat enough at one meal to last through the day, and so should be fed at least twice a day; preferably more often, but not to excess. Live foods that live on for a time can be very useful if you cannot manage frequent feeding, or an automatic feeder may be installed. There are also some preparations on the market that are claimed not to pollute the water if left in it for several days to be picked at by the fishes. These are the so-called "vacation blocks."

When feeding normally, remember the time-honored rule to feed only as much as is consumed within five minutes, and to syphon off any that remains. So watch the fishes as you feed them, see that all are getting some and stop within five minutes or when any food is being left uneaten. Don't dump in all at once, particularly when

using dry food, as it swells in the stomach if gobbled down rapidly. As a guide, the average 2″ fish does well on 10 mg dry food (1/300 th oz approx.!) per feed if fed twice daily. This is only about 1/2 oz per week per 100 fishes, so your flakes should last quite a time.

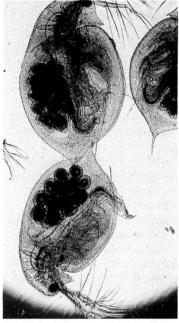

Adult female Daphnia. *Photo by Fritz Siedel.*

If you are away for up to a week, leave the fishes unfed; for a longer period get somebody to feed them. A fellow aquarist is much the safest, but if a kind neighbor is to do the job, leave a daily package with strict instructions never to feed anything else. People unaccustomed to aquaria seem always to overfeed grossly if left to their own devices.

Diseases and Parasites

Most aquarium keepers have only one tank, although I expect that those who are likely to buy books on the subject are also likely to have more than one. Even so, they are still unlikely to have a quarantine tank and so whenever possible the recommendations in this chapter will involve treatment of the whole aquarium when trouble occurs. This raises a problem—nobody wants to dose a tank with anything that is going to kill plants or helpful bacteria, or to stain everything or color the water deeply. Various antibiotics and dyes will therefore only be recommended if nothing else is known to be effective.

When medication is used in an aquarium, carbon filters must be turned off, so must resin-containing filters and similar pads must be removed. These all remove the drug from the water and can be used for that purpose when a cure has been effected. Biological filters cannot be turned off for long, but may need to be turned down and given rest periods if certain drugs, particularly antibiotics, have to be employed. Then, aeration must be turned to a maximum to offset the lack of adequate filtration and water movement.

Naturally, we are only going to observe external symptoms when a fish is in an aquarium and few of us will be in a position to examine a fish further for diagnostic purposes, even when it is dead. So, unless expert advice is sought, we have to rely

A red swordtail showing exophthalmus or pop-eye.

on what we can see and to treat accordingly. When in doubt, a combination of treatments can be given, after taking the precaution of seeing how well they mix in a jar of water before using them. If no precipitate, cloudiness or color change occurs, they are probably safe together. Many commercial remedies use such mixtures and if one can be found that contains the recommended drugs or chemicals in about the right dosage, use it if you wish.

Here is a table of some common symptoms and the conditions they probably indicate, as a guide to treatment:

Symptoms	Probable Causes
Small white spots on fins or skin	*Ichthyophthirius* (white spot or ich)
Yellowish, tiny spots, often moving, on fins or skin.	*Oodinium* (Velvet)
Glancing off plants or decorations, fins clamped	Either of the above; toxins
Gray or white fluffy patches	*Saprolegnia* or *Achlya* (fungus)
Similar patches only around mouth	*Chondrococcus* (mouth fungus)
Colors fading beneath the skin	*Plistophora* ("neon disease")
Reddish or black nodules under the skin	*Metacercaria* (digenetic Flukes)
Milky cloudiness on surface of skin	*Costia, Chilodonella, Trichodina* or pH too extreme
Red streaks on skin or fins	Red pest (bacterial)
Destruction of tail or fins	Tail or fin rot (bacterial)
Ulcerated patches on skin	Red pest or *Ichthyosporidium*
Yellow to black nodules on or below skin	*Ichthyosporidium*
Emaciation, hollow belly, possibly sores	Tuberculosis or *Hexamita*
Protrusion of scales with swollen body	Dropsy (*Aeromonas* infection)
Protrusion of scales, often red, body normal	Bacterial infection of scales
Pop-eye (exophthalmos)	Gas embolism, copper poisoning, sometimes various diseases
Cloudy eyes, blindness	Severe white spot or velvet; toxins
Holes in head, lateral line affected sometimes	*Hexamita* or viral
Crustaceans on skin	*Argulus*, copepods
Flukes (often like white spot) visible on skin or gills	*Gyrodactylus*, other monogenetic flukes
Worms hanging from anus	*Nematoda*
Nodular white swellings on fins or body, "cauliflower" tumors	*Lymphocystis* (a virus), *Glugea* or *Henneguya* (sporozoans)
Spinal deformity	Hereditary, vitamin or calcium lack, Tuberculosis, *Ichthyosporidium*
Sluggish, loss of balance	*Trypanoplasma* (sleeping sickness), water too cold, other possible causes
Severe loss of balance	Swim bladder disease
Gasping at surface	Oxygen lack, CO_2 excess, water too hot, toxins
Sudden dashes, jumping from water	Wrong pH, toxins

Viral Diseases

Viruses are minute infectors of cells that they depend upon for reproduction, being unable to multiply outside them. Very little is known about viral diseases in fishes, and no sure cures are available.

This headstander has tail rot.

Lymphocystis virus causes cells to swell up enormously, giving rise to white, spawn-like masses or irregular tumors on the fins or body. It is best to destroy an infected fish before others catch the disease, which is rarely fatal but very disfiguring. Luckily it is not a very common disease in freshwater fishes.

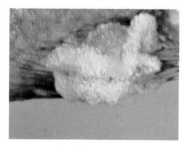

This fish is showing Lymphocystis *virus disease.*

Bacterial Diseases

Bacteria are legion, and the particular one causing trouble can usually only be guessed at unless laboratory tests are made. However, we know from experience the probable culprit in various conditions.

Red pest, fin and *tail rot* and ulcerations may all be caused by various bacteria, almost always gram-negative strains that are resistant to penicillin (although

not to some of the new derivatives). Light infections may be treated with a good clean-up of the tank, together with disinfection. For this purpose, acriflavine (trypaflavine) or monacrin (monoamino-acridine) are best, using 0.2% stock solution at up to 1 ml per gallon (1 standard teaspoon per 5 gallons). The yellowish or blueish tinge they give to the water is not offensive, and as it fades the treatment may be repeated, usually in 2–3 days.

If the above is not effective, or the condition is bad to begin with, substitute an antibiotic given by mouth, in the food. Keep the fishes hungry and feed lightly twice a day on flakes or other dry food mixed with up to 1% of chloromycetin (chloramphenicol). A 250 mg capsule in 1 oz of food is about right, thoroughly mixed. This amount will not affect biological filters even if not eaten, but gives the fishes an effective dosage. It can if necessary be given with fresh foods instead. If the fishes are not eating, as a last resort give the drug at 50 mg per gallon in the water, but then problems of effects on biological filters and resistant strains being encouraged occur.

Other antibiotics than chloromycetin may be tried, but it would be my own first choice as it is widely effective and rarely used except in ear-drops, etc., in human medicine. Tetracyclines, kanamycin or gentamycin are possibilities, or ampicillin or one of the other new and widely active penicillin derivatives.

Mouth fungus looks like its name, but is caused by a bacterium, *Chondrococcus columnaris*, that grows out in fluffy tufts. It looks at first like a white line around the mouth and later fluffs out. It is very toxic and as the fishes cannot usually eat, it should be treated,

This angelfish has mouth fungus.

exceptionally, with antibiotic in the water. Penicillin is effective at 40,000 units per gallon, with a second dose after 2 days. Chloromycetin at 50 mg per gallon may be used instead. A cure should result in 4–5 days.

Tuberculosis is caused by the bacterium *Mycobacterium piscium*, a relative of human tuberculosis. Symptoms are "knife-back," or "razor-back" due to muscle wasting, hollow belly, pale skin and in later stages, ulcers and ragged fins. No reliable treatment has been found and infected fishes should be destroyed and the aquarium disinfected or at least cleaned up as far as possible.

Dropsy, swelling of the body with consequent scale protrusion, is also bacterial and usually caused by kidney disease, commonly by *Aeromonas (Pseudomonas) punctata*. Chloromycetin or other antibiotic in the food as already described should be administered, but there is no certainty of a cure.

Scale protrusion without body swelling is due to a surface infection, although the condition may be more general. It can be caused by a variety of bacteria and should be treated with antibiotic in the food. Again, a general clean-up should accompany any such treatment.

This goldfish has scale protrusion.

Diseases and Parasites

Protozoal Diseases

Protozoa are one-celled animals, often parasitic on fishes and the cause of the two most frequently recognized diseases, velvet and white spot.

Velvet, or rust disease, is caused by several species of *Oodinium*, all with similar life histories. They have a free-swimming stage that settles down on the fish or in the gills and attaches itself to the skin, often waving gently at first, finally forming a cyst and either falling off the fish or remaining on it, in both cases releasing several hundred new free-swimmers. Infected fishes are clearly irritated, glance off decorations and respire rapidly due to gill congestion, yet the disease is often difficult to see. Careful inspection, preferably at an angle to the surface of the fish, will show a powdery, yellowish infestation.

The best treatment is copper, at a maximum of 0.4 ppm, best given in divided doses on two successive days. If using copper sulphate, which is only 20% metallic copper, 2 ppm should be given, 0.8 ml per gallon (1 standard teaspoon per six gallons) of a 1% solution in distilled water in 2 divided doses 12 hours apart. A half dose may be given in another 3 days if a cure is not apparent, but the parasites on the fishes will not disappear rapidly, as it is the free-living stage that is affected primarily. Heat, up to 80°F, is a help as it hastens development of the cysts.

Acriflavine (trypaflavine) may be substituted for copper, using a stock solution of 0.2% and adding up to 1 ml per gallon (1 standard teaspoon per 5 gallons). The addition of a teaspoon of salt per gallon helps its action, and more acriflavine may be added as the yellowish color in the water fades.

White spot is caused by the protozoan *Ichthyophthirius multifiliis*, hence the common name "Ich." It is up to $1/25''$ diameter and so causes bigger spots than velvet. It has a free-swimming stage that settles down on the skin and gills and burrows in to become covered by a layer of cells that form a cyst—the white spot. After several days it finds its way out again and falls from the fish, forms a cyst itself which eventually frees about 1,000 young that seek new hosts. The cycle takes from a month at 68°F to only 5 days at 80°F.

The free-swimming stage is susceptible to treatment, but the cysts in the fish resist it. The fishes are restless, glancing off rocks and plants and respiring rapidly as with velvet, so the diagnosis depends on the spots. Copper is not a cure. The temperature should be raised to shorten the cycle and the drug of choice is quinine hydrochloride, but the sulphate may be used instead. Treat at 2 grains per gallon (30 mg per liter) by dissolving the total dose in a pint or two of water and add it to the tank one third at a time at 12-hour intervals. Increase aeration, turn off carbon filters and wait and see. Spots on the fishes should disappear over the next few days and not reappear. If they do, repeat the treatment, but only if really necessary as a second dose can be hard on some plants and fishes. One treatment does not need other than routine water changes, but two require more frequent changes after a cure is effected.

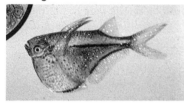

This silver hatchetfish shows ich or white spot.

Another frequently recommended treatment is malachite green (zinc free) at 1 drop per gallon of a 0.75% solution. It is used for cheapness, but tetras cannot tolerate it and it stains plastics and silicones. In the case of anabantids and other fishes that can stand high temperatures and low oxygen, heat alone in the 90°F range will kill the parasites that cannot stand these conditions.

Costia necatrix causes skin cloudiness and appears to live on the skin permanently, multiplying on the fish. A temperature of 86°–90°F also kills it and as aeration can be

This neon tetra has Plistophora *or neon disease.*

freely used, most fishes can take it for a couple of days. Otherwise, treat with acriflavine as for velvet.

Hexamita is often associated with "hole-in-the-head" disease, which looks as if bits of the head region and sometimes the lateral line have been gouged out. If due to *Hexamita*, metranidazole (Flagyl®) is the drug of choice, as a combined treatment of 1% in the food and ⅔ grain per gallon in the water (12 mg per liter).

Trypanoplasma causes sleeping sickness in fishes that become drowsy, emaciated and may swim abnormally. There is no cure and infected fishes should be destroyed.

This discus fish has "hole in the head" Hexamita.

Chilodonella causes a blue-white cloudiness and later may attack the gills and cause skin ulcerations. The fishes show much the same behavior as for velvet. Treatment with acriflavine

121

Diseases and Parasites

These dead neons have lost most of their fins and are wasted away from fish tuberculosis.

Saprolegnia and *Achlya* are examples of such fungi. They form a network under the skin surface and eventually send out tufts of *hyphae* looking like cotton wool. These produce swimming spores that infect other fishes if they too are weak or injured. Untreated, fungus can kill. If only one or two fishes are affected, it is best to net them out and treat them with a brief fungicidal bath of malachite green (zinc free) at 4 grains per gallon (60 mg per liter approx.). Usually a single bath is enough, but the treatment can be

is recommended, but at a concentration of up to 20 ml (1 tablespoon) of the 0.2% stock solution per gallon, with a change of water afterwards.

Plistophora, the cause of "neon tetra disease" causes white patches beneath the skin that obscure colors. It attacks other species than neons and as there is no cure, affected fishes should be destroyed.

Glugea and *Henneguya* are similar protozoans causing large cysts that may appear anywhere in or on the fishes. Once more, no cure is known and to avoid further spread, affected fishes should be destroyed.

Fungal Diseases

Fungi are plants, lacking the characteristic green pigment of other plants. External fungi usually only attack weakened or damaged fishes and their spores fall into the aquarium from the air so that permanent eradication is impossible.

This archerfish has a fungus infection of Saprolegnia.

repeated. The *hyphae* are stained green and drop off in a few hours; those below the skin die off. If a lot of fishes are affected, it may be easier to treat the tank, when phenoxethol is used. A 1% solution in distilled water is added at 40 ml (2 tablespoons) per gallon, repeated only once if necessary. Phenoxethol is an oily liquid sparingly soluble in water. It is hard to find in many areas.

Ichthyosporidium (Ichthyophonus) hoferi is a widespread internal fungus attacking first the liver and kidneys but later spreading anywhere. Infection occurs via the gut. The fungus invades the bloodstream and causes brown cysts up to $1/10''$ in size. Symptoms are variable, from sluggishness, hollow belly, loss of balance, to death. The cause only becomes apparent in the living fish when the cysts occur externally, by which time it is too late to hope for a cure. Phenoxethol added to the food as a 1% solution, also added to the water as above, can be tried to save the spread of the condition to other fishes, but obviously infected fishes should be killed. Luckily, in good conditions, early infection can be limited and the cysts isolated within the tissues.

Worms

Various worms cause trouble in the aquarium, of which the most important are the flukes.

Flukes (trematodes) infesting fishes are usually those passed from fish to fish and not, as do many, requiring intermediate hosts such as snails or birds. There are many species and genera; those usually mentioned are *Gyrodactylus, Dactylogyrus* and *Monocoelium*. These are all quite small, up to $1/25''$ in length and easily mistaken for white spot, infesting gills and skin. A lens shows the difference—look for movement and two black eye-spots. The response of the fishes is also similar to that of white spot, irritation and rapid respiration, later emaciation. All are treated alike, if feasible by a bath of up to 30 minutes in $2/3$ grain per gallon (10 mg per liter) of potassium permanganate, or by treatment of the whole tank with 2 mg per liter, but this is a messy method as the chemical is deep purple in color and then precipitates as a brown sludge. Otherwise, formalin as a 45 minute bath may be used—but not in the tank. A bath of 1 teaspoon (5 ml) of a 40% solution per 7 gallons of water is effective. As an easy cure if it works (depending on the species of fluke), is a 20 minute bath in $1/2$ strength sea water or 2 oz per gallon of common salt. Trichlorofon (Neguvon Bayer) at 0.25 ppm is a new treatment in the aquarium that reputedly works in a single dose that dissipates naturally.

To avoid diseases caused by other flukes that have intermediate hosts, inspect fishes carefully before purchase and never introduce snails into the aquarium that are not guaranteed tank bred.

Threadworms (nematodes) and *Tapeworms* (cestodes) will rarely be detected, and are normally not dangerous, even though they are common inhabitants of the gut.

Crustaceans

There are two crustaceans of importance in the aquarium:

Argulus, the fish louse and *Lernae*, the anchor worm, a copepod.

Argulus species are quite large, $1/5''$–$2/5''$ in size and can be picked off with forceps. The parasite attaches itself to the fish by two large suckers and feeds on its blood. It is also poisonous and a rapid breeder. Treatments recommended are potassium permanganate, or Trichlorofon (Neguvon Bayer) that reputedly work as well for *Argulus* as for flukes, at the same concentrations.

Lernaea cyprinacea is a copepod that buries its head in the skin and has two trailing egg sacs up to nearly 1″ long, the "worms." The male is not parasitic. The parasite cannot be pulled out and treatment with permanganate as for *Argulus*, or with DFD (difluoro-diphenyl-trichloromethylmethane), a liquid, may be used in a bath at 1 teaspoon per 12 gallons (1 ml per 10 liters) for 2–3 minutes, but not in the aquarium. However, young adults may not be affected and you must look out for the need of repeated treatments.

Exophthalmos

"Pop-eye" is not caused by any one agent, but is commonly associated with excess of gases in the blood, as when water is introduced under high pressure. It can also occur in association with dropsy or *Ichthyosporidium*. If bubbles are seen in the eye, lower the temperature as far as possible (68°F is usually safe) and decrease any brisk aeration. Pop-eye may also be hormonal, in which case it may disappear spontaneously.

Wrong pH, Toxins

Both a high or a low pH for any particular species may cause gill injury, cloudy skin and gasping at the surface or jumping out. A check should be made whenever these symptoms occur. The same symptoms can occur with toxins or overheated tanks. A low pH can be associated with carbon dioxide excess, with the need for a very brisk aeration and a part-water change.

Toxins of various types can cause a variety of symptoms. Metallic poisoning tends to cause cloudy eyes and inflamed skin or fins, when all possible causes should be investigated if no disease is apparent. Copper piping is a common culprit. Chloramine in tap water, sprays of all kinds near a tank are suspect, as is new paint or any source of ammonia. Phenolic compounds can be released by cheap plastics, dying tubifex or some types of algae, even by uneaten food. When any such trouble is suspected progressive water changes and a good clean-up should be commenced and thought given to the possible causes.

Your local aquarium store should be most familiar with diseases and their remedies. Consult them frequently if you have problems. As a general rule a sick fish is best disposed of.

Suggested Reading

The following books published by T.F.H. Publications are available at pet shops and book stores everywhere.

Dr. Axelrod's Atlas of Freshwater Aquarium Fishes
By Dr. Herbert R. Axelrod, Dr. Warren E. Burgess, Neal Pronek, and Jerry G. Walls.
ISBN 0-86622-052-6
T.F.H. H-1077
The ultimate aquarium book—illustrated with over 4000 color photos. Almost every fish available to hobbyists is illustrated! Species are grouped geographically and by family for easy reference. No aquarist's library is complete without it!

Exotic Tropical Fishes Expanded Edition
By Dr. Herbert R. Axelrod, Dr. C. W. Emmens, Dr. Warren E. Burgess, and Neal Pronek.
ISBN 0-87666-543-1 (hardcover),
ISBN 0-87666-537-7 (looseleaf)
T.F.H. H-1028 (hardcover),
H-1028L (looseleaf)
The "bible" of freshwater ornamental fishes—contains comprehensive information on aquarium maintenance, plants, and commercial culture, as well as over 1,000 color photos and entries on many hundreds of species. New supplements are issued every month in *Tropical Fish Hobbyist* magazine, and may be placed into the looseleaf edition.

Index

CO-029 S

TROPICAL FISH

A COMPLETE INTRODUCTION

Dr. Cliff W. Emmens